Ten Real Tools For Real Life:

Essential Tools For Emotional Health

Developed by Susan Hansen, M.S.

National Library of Canada Cataloguing in Publication

Hansen, Susan, 1963-
    Ten real tools for real life / Susan Hansen.

ISBN 1-55369-795-2

    I. Title.

HQ2037.H35 2002   646.7   C2002-903570-8

TRAFFORD

This book was published *on-demand* in cooperation with Trafford Publishing.
On-demand publishing is a unique process and service of making a book available for retail sale to the public taking advantage of on-demand manufacturing and Internet marketing.
On-demand publishing includes promotions, retail sales, manufacturing, order fulfilment, accounting and collecting royalties on behalf of the author.

Suite 6E, 2333 Government St., Victoria, B.C. V8T 4P4, CANADA
Phone   250-383-6864   Toll-free   1-888-232-4444 (Canada & US)
Fax   250-383-6804   E-mail   sales@trafford.com
Web site   www.trafford.com   TRAFFORD PUBLISHING IS A DIVISION OF TRAFFORD HOLDINGS LTD.
Trafford Catalogue #02-0608   www.trafford.com/robots/02-0608.html

10   9   8   7   6   5   4   3   2

TABLE OF CONTENTS:

ABOUT THIS WORKBOOK AND THESE TOOLS:

This is the workbook I desperately needed in 8th grade, and it wasn't there.

If you're reading this, chances are that like me, you've probably sat in classrooms somewhere (maybe recently, maybe not) and learned language, math, science, and social studies, in one form or another. You've probably learned from textbooks, worksheets, videos, projects, and lots of classroom instruction. Chances are also good that you've wondered -- at least once -- when you were ever going to use some pieces of information, or why there weren't more classes offered that applied in some more personal, practical way to your daily life.

I'm not trying to insult schools or education -- I've been a teacher (high school English and drama) and counselor (K-8 intervention specialist and private practice counselor, among other things) since 1986. But ever since I was in 8th grade, having a truly miserable year and not getting any real help, I've wondered why no one offered classes in the basic skills of dealing with myself, my feelings, my life, and my relationships with other people.

I never heard a really good answer to that question. So, after many years of trial and error, learning and practice, I created and began teaching classes like these, both in schools and in my private practice. Over the years I developed a set of ten tools, and then taught them to everyone who would let me. At the request of several groups of students, I included them in a book I wrote called *Tools For Your Emotional Health Toolbox*, which is still available and is mostly used by counselors. After several more requests, I put together this workbook, which can be used by teenagers or adults on their own, with family members or a friend, with a counselor, or with a group.

So, this is the book I wish I'd had in 8th grade. It offers ten basic tools -- and I know there are hundreds of useful tools out there, but these ten build a good strong foundation. So whether you're somewhere near 8th grade or way past that time, I hope this workbook is helpful to you. As with any other tools, if you learn to use them correctly, and practice using them on a regular basis, they really do work, and you'll be amazed at the life you can build with them.

THE TEN BASIC TOOLS -- AN OVERVIEW:

Let me make it clear that I didn't invent most of these tools. Many of them have been around for quite awhile in various forms. What I did was put them into a format that could be easily learned and practiced, and organized and refined them in a way that made sense to me.

Once you learn and practice these ten tools, you will be more skilled at dealing with your own feelings and communicating with others than most people in the world. This may sound like an outrageous statement, but I think it's true. The majority of people are not taught these skills, but those who are have a great advantage -- not because they're better than anyone else, but because they're more aware and more comfortable with themselves and in dealing with other people. These skills are priceless.

1. "I" STATEMENTS:

Learn this simple tool and begin to express yourself more clearly, reduce arguing, blaming, and defensiveness, keep tempers from flaring, focus on solutions rather than problems, and save time and energy.

2. DAILY CHECK-IN:

Do this brief daily check-in on your own and/or with others to practice using "I" statements, identify and express your experiences, thoughts, and feelings, and form real connections with other people, and with yourself.

3. DEFENSES:

Learn how you usually defend yourself against stress, fear, and pain. Identify which specific defenses you use, and learn how they affect you and your relationships. Decide which defenses are no longer useful to you, and learn how to let them go and what to do instead.

4. WHAT'S UNDER ANGER:

Learn how anger, hurt, fear, and other feelings go together, and how to sort out all your feelings about a situation, identify your needs, take steps toward resolving the situation, and take care of yourself no matter what.

5. SUPPORTIVE FEEDBACK:

Learn to offer support to someone else without giving advice or trying to fix the situation. Practice your listening skills, use your "I" statements again, and learn to validate what the other person is feeling -- a far more useful and helpful skill than having all the answers.

6. THE RAGE BOMB:

Learn how anger and rage are different, and what all the components of rage are. Identify your own rage triggers and behaviors, and learn how to diffuse the bomb before it explodes.

7. COMMUNICATION STYLES:

Learn the difference between aggressive, passive, passive-aggressive and assertive behaviors and communication styles. Identify which styles you typically use, the pros and cons of each style, the benefits for you of becoming more assertive, and how to get there.

8. BOUNDARIES:

Learn what healthy boundaries are, why we need them, and how to clearly set and maintain them. Use the step-by-step process to stand up for yourself and keep your power, even if the other person doesn't cooperate.

9. THE DRAMA TRIANGLE:

Learn the unproductive roles people play in most conflicts, how to identify which roles you and others are playing, and how to get out of the triangle and stay balanced, no matter what anyone else is doing.

10: HEALTHY OUTLETS FOR ANGER AND STRESS:

Learn what separates healthy venting from being destructive or harmful, and identify dozens of healthy outlets (in several different categories) that you can use when you're angry or stressed.

HOW TO USE THIS WORKBOOK FOR BEST RESULTS:

This part is simple:

1. Don't just read the workbook -- do the activities! Get your pen or pencil, and every time there's a question, WRITE DOWN the answer. Every time there's a worksheet, do it! (Don't worry, there are blank copies in the back of the book of worksheets you might want to do again. Find a copy machine and have at it.) This is your workbook. Circle things, highlight things, write in the margins. Reading the workbook and not doing the activities is like looking into a toolbox and believing you are now qualified to build a house. The only way the tools will be useful for you is to use and practice them.

2. Do all of the tools in order. Start with #1 and work your way to #10. Don't skip any, because they all build on each other.

3. If you do this work alone, it will benefit you - to a certain point. However, whenever possible, share your answers with someone - a trusted friend, family member, teacher, or counselor. If you can do this work with a group or in a class, that's even better. Some of these tools are about how you communicate with other people, and the only real way to practice them is with other people.

4. If you work with other people, set up your confidentiality guidelines ahead of time, commit to them, and follow them. The basic confidentiality agreement states: "What is said and done here, stays here." The exceptions are:

   A) If someone is in **imminent, life-threatening danger** -- planning to harm or has already harmed him/herself or someone else. Situations like suicide plans or attempts, self-induced cutting or burning, drug overdose, eating disorders, and runaway plans fall into this category. Other things may too -- use your best judgment (better an ex-friend than a dead friend, I always say). Call a parent, teacher, counselor, or other trusted adult, and if you don't know who else to call, call 911.

   B) If **physical or sexual abuse** of a minor by an adult is reported. Educators and counselors are required by law to report this to Child Protective Services and/or the police. Again, even if you aren't required to do so, please tell a trusted adult.

SUGGESTED GUIDELINES FOR GROUP WORK:

If you are a counselor or group facilitator, I would suggest having a written set of guidelines and expectations for members of the group, beyond the confidentiality guidelines on the previous page. You may already have your own, but if not, feel free to use these:

1. All beliefs are treated with respect.

2. No "putdowns" to self or others -- even as a joke.

3. Everyone has the right to pass.

4. Everyone's participation is important.

5. Be on time.

6. No side talk or cross talk.

7. Use "I" statements -- speak only for yourself.

8. No "shoulds" toward yourself or others.

9. Confidentiality: What is said in group stays in group.

[Clarify Exceptions to Confidentiality (see previous page)]:

If you are not a counselor: I would also recommend having these agreements in place if you are doing work with a friend, group of friends, teacher, etc. I would encourage you to make **very specific and clear agreements** before you start, so the expectations and responsibilities of everyone involved are clear.

If you would like more guidelines for setting up groups, and detailed lesson plans for these and many other related activities, you can find them in Tools For Your Emotional Health Toolbox, a manual I wrote for counselors and support group facilitators. If you'd like more information about this book, please see my contact information on page 103.

Best wishes and enjoy the journey!

TOOL #1: "I" STATEMENTS

Overview:

Learn this simple tool and begin to express yourself more clearly, reduce arguing, blaming, and defensiveness, keep tempers from flaring, focus on solutions rather than problems, and save time and energy.

Getting Started:

Think of someone you know (past or present) who tends to argue, yell, or blame, uses the word "you" a lot instead of "I," or tells you what to do. Who is the person, and what is an example of the behavior?

My Examples:

-- A student about a teacher: "She gave me an 'F' -- she just doesn't like me."
-- A brother to a sister: "You cheated! That's not fair!"
-- A mother to a grown daughter: "Don't you want to get your doctorate?"

Your Example(s):

Information on "I" Statements:

"I" statements are a basic communication skill that may seem obvious or simplistic when you first learn them, but they are actually very powerful. Their power lies in **ownership**, teaching us to take responsibility for our own thoughts, feelings, opinions, and behaviors. **If we take responsibility for something, then we have choices.** If we blame or give away our power to other people (more on that later), we give away our choices and feel stuck.

Ten Real Tools For Real Life by Susan Hansen, M.S. copyright 2002, 2006. All Rights Reserved.

"I" statements serve several purposes:

-- They help reduce blaming and arguing.
-- They help reduce defensive responses from the other person.
-- They help keep the focus on solutions rather than problems.
-- They help keep tempers from flaring.
-- They save time and are an effective use of time.

The basic "I" statement includes any of the following:

When you _____, I feel _____.
When you _____, I felt _____.   (OR)

I feel _____ when you _____.
I felt _____ when you _____.

It's important to have the "feeling" component in the statement, both so that you can acknowledge and take ownership for what you feel, and because **feelings are harder to argue with than opinions**. Use actual feeling words, such as "angry," "frustrated," "worried," etc., rather than "feel like" or "feel that" statements ("I feel like hurting you," or "I feel that you're being selfish"). Those are actually **thoughts** disguised as feelings, and they're major argument starters.

It's also important to **leave out judgments of any kind**. Saying, "I feel frustrated" will trigger far fewer arguments than saying, "I feel like you don't care about me." (Saying that the person doesn't care about me is my opinion, and is a judgment.) If I say someone is "selfish," I am judging that person or the behavior. But if I say that the person has been late four times in a row, I'm stating what happened without making any judgments.

Here are some general examples of "I" statements:

-- "**When you** interrupt me, **I feel** frustrated and annoyed."
-- "**When you** laughed at me in front of everyone, **I felt** humiliated."
-- "**I feel** uncomfortable **when you** stand close to me when we're talking."
-- "**I felt** worried **when you** didn't call to let me know where you were."

-- "I disagree with you," instead of, "You're wrong."
-- "I'm afraid you don't care about me," instead of, "You don't care."

<u>"I" Statement Practice:</u>

Most people don't use "I" statements when they talk in everyday conversation. To get the feel for using them, consider events in your life lately, look at the following partial statements, and fill them in so they're true for you. Remember to use real feeling words, and leave out judgments:

I feel angry when _____.

I feel frustrated when _____.

I felt worried when _____.

I feel lonely when _____.

I felt happy when _____.

I felt loved when _____.

I feel peaceful when _____.

When someone is late, I feel _____.

When someone breaks a promise to me, I feel _____.

When I get interrupted, I feel _____.

When I argue with _____, I feel _____.

When _____ gets angry, I feel _____.

<u>Categories of Statements:</u>

Here are some categories of statements people use instead of "I" statements, followed by examples of "I" statements that could be used instead:

JUDGMENT STATEMENTS

He's a _____.   "I" statement: I get so furious
                                       when he _____.

You're being a _____.   "I" statement: When you _____,
                                       I feel _____.

THREATS

She'd better watch her back.   "I" statement: I've had it with her.

I'm going to kick your _____.   "I" statement: I feel _____
                                              when _____.

ASSUMPTIONS

(These are tricky because they can contain the word "I.")

She doesn't like me.   "I" statement: I don't think she likes me.
                                   (OR) I'm afraid she doesn't like me.

I know he would never lie to me.   "I" statement: I trust him. (OR)
                                   I don't think he'd lie to me.

ACCUSATIONS

You've been talking behind my back. "I" statement: I heard that you said _____
                                   about me. Is that true?

He took money out of my room.   "I" statement: I'm afraid that he took it. (OR)
                                        I need to find out if he took it.

ATTACKING INSTEAD OF ASKING

Why are you telling all my secrets? "I" statement: Have you told anyone what I
                                   told you in private?

What's wrong with you anyway?   "I" statement: I don't understand what
you're

doing. What's going on?

GIVING AWAY POWER*

You make me sick.   "I" statement: I feel _____ when
                                     you _____.

She makes me so mad.   "I" statement: I get so mad when
                                     she_____.

*Note: If I say that someone else "makes" me sick or angry or upset, I'm basically giving that person the power to do that. I actually have power over my own feelings (or I can learn to have it), but if I give it away, I'm saying that any outside person or situation can "make" me feel something, and I don't have my own power.

If I say, "I'm so frustrated!" instead of "You make me so mad," at least I have choices. I can vent the anger. I can take steps to change the situation. I can talk to someone and ask for support. But if I let another person "make" me feel something, I'm essentially giving up my power, and other people can have control of my world any time they want to. Also, some people enjoy feeling that they can "make" me angry, and will do it often, just to get the response. It doesn't have to be that way

Practice Changing Other Statements Into "I" Statements:

Read the following statements, and:

A. Identify any judgment words or other argument-triggering words (like "always" and "never." Circle or underline these words.

B. Rewrite the statement as an "I" statement, and remember to include feeling words (not "feel like" or "feel that") whenever you can.

ORIGINAL STATEMENT: "You're always late."

"I" STATEMENT: _____

_____

ORIGINAL STATEMENT: "If you respected me, you wouldn't yell at me all the time."

"I" STATEMENT: _____

_____

ORIGINAL STATEMENT: "Your constant interrupting is rude and annoying."

"I" STATEMENT: _____

_____

ORIGINAL STATEMENT: "She makes me sick with all her whining."

"I" STATEMENT: _____

_____

ORIGINAL STATEMENT: "Why do you have to argue with everything I say?"

"I" STATEMENT: _____

_____

(Some sample "I" statements for the above exercises are on page 14, but there are many right answers.)

Now think of some non-"I" statements that you have said or heard. First write down the original statement, then rewrite it as an "I" statement. This is good practice for using this tool in your own life.

ORIGINAL STATEMENT: _____

_____

"I" STATEMENT: _____

_____

ORIGINAL STATEMENT: _____

_____

"I" STATEMENT: _____

_____

ORIGINAL STATEMENT: _____

_____

"I" STATEMENT: _____

_____

ORIGINAL STATEMENT: _____

_____

"I" STATEMENT: _____

_____

Closure/Practice:

Using "I" statements takes practice -- lots of it. Name one person you get frustrated with (or one situation, such as a workplace or classroom) where you will practice using "I" statements over the next few weeks:

_____

_____

Is It Yours Yet?

Be prepared to answer (either verbally or in writing) the following questions about "I" statements. The information isn't really yours until you can clearly explain or teach it to someone else.

1. Name three benefits of using "I" statements.
2. What does this statement mean?: "The power of 'I' statements lies in ownership."
3. What kinds of problems can occur when we give away our power?
4. How does using "I" statements help us keep our power?
5. Give an example of a basic "I" statement.
6. Why is it important to have the "feeling" component in an "I" statement?
7. Why is it important to leave judgment words out of "I" statements?

Possible answers for the practice exercise on pages 11-12:

ORIGINAL STATEMENT: "You're always late."

"I" STATEMENT: "I feel frustrated and annoyed when you're late," or "I feel frustrated and annoyed when we agree to meet at a certain time and you're not there."

ORIGINAL STATEMENT: "If you really respected me, you wouldn't yell at me all the time."

"I" STATEMENT: "I feel hurt and uncomfortable when you yell," or "I feel hurt and uncomfortable when you raise your voice with me."

ORIGINAL STATEMENT: "Your constant interrupting is rude and annoying."

"I" STATEMENT: "When you interrupt me, I feel frustrated and violated," or "When you start talking before I finish my sentence, I feel frustrated and violated."

ORIGINAL STATEMENT: "She makes me sick with all her whining."

"I" STATEMENT: "I feel angry and impatient when I hear her whining," or "I feel angry and impatient when I hear her talking in that tone of voice."

ORIGINAL STATEMENT: "Why do you have to argue with everything I say?"

"I" STATEMENT: "I feel frustrated and discouraged when I tell you things and you disagree, especially when it happens several times in one conversation."

TOOL #2: DAILY CHECK-IN

Overview:

Do this brief daily check-in on your own and/or with others to practice using "I" statements, identify and express your experiences, thoughts, and feelings, and form real connections with other people, and with yourself.

About Doing a Daily Check-in:

Now that you know about "I" statements, you can practice using them so they become more automatic, and to get more comfortable using feeling words. Most people who use any feeling words at all stick to the basics: happy, sad, mad, or scared. Others say they feel "good," "okay," "bad," or "fine" -- and none of those are really feelings. The daily check-in helps expand your feelings vocabulary, so you can know yourself better and communicate more clearly to other people.

Check-in Format:

Here's the basic format -- it's simple and brief, but very powerful:

1. A low point for me today was _____...
2. ... and I felt _____.
3. A high point for me today was _____...
4. ... and I felt _____.

Examples:

An average day: "A low point for me today was that I didn't have enough money to buy the CD I wanted, and I felt frustrated and discouraged. A high point was that I talked to my mom this morning without arguing with her, and I felt relieved and glad.

A difficult day: "A low point for me today was that my boyfriend broke up with me, and I felt devastated and betrayed. The only high point I can think of for today was that my friends were supportive, and I felt grateful."

A great day: A high point today is that I got the job I interviewed for, and I feel excited and hopeful, because I really wanted it. A low point today is that I know it's going to be a lot of hard work, and I feel scared that I might not be able to do it well."

<u>Things to Consider:</u>

-- You can do the low point or high point first if you want to -- the order doesn't matter.

-- You can use more than one feeling word for each situation; in fact, try to use two or three for each.

-- Remember to say "I felt" or "I feel," not "It made me feel" (remember, this is how you keep your power).

-- Remember that "good," "bad," "fine," etc. are not really feeling words, and neither are "feel like" or "feel that" statements, which are more thoughts than feelings.

-- Don't worry if your topics aren't earth-shaking. It's good practice to note the small highs and lows in your life too.

-- Pick both a high point and a low point every time you do check-in. Unless you're unconscious, there will be many high points and low points in any given day. Identifying both helps you keep your balance.

-- If you're doing check-in with another person or group, remember and honor your agreements about confidentiality.

<u>Categories of Feelings and Feeling Words:</u>

Here are some feeling words to get you started. You can always add your own if you think of more:

<u>HAPPINESS</u>	<u>ANGER</u>	<u>HURT</u>
hopeful	mad	sad
peaceful	frustrated	let down
relieved	enraged	depressed
excited	irritated	lonely/left out
loved	annoyed	devastated
relaxed	disgusted	violated
connected	aggravated	betrayed

FEAR	GUILT	SHAME	LONELINESS
worried	mad at myself	stupid	left out
stressed	responsible	embarrassed	rejected
overwhelmed	pressured	humiliated	unwanted
rejected	overwhelmed	belittled	alone
terrified	remorse	ugly	isolated
anxious	regret	powerless	misunderstood
afraid	sorrow	not good enough	outcast

Written Check-Ins:

Whether you're learning these tools on your own or with others, doing a written check-in is valuable. It's the easiest and quickest form of journaling around, and helps you keep track of progress, patterns, and the events and feelings in your life. Take a few minutes and do these written check-ins:

During the past 24 hours:

1. A low point for me was _____

_____...

2. ... and I felt _____.

3. A high point for me was _____

_____...

4. ... and I felt _____.

During the past week or two:

1. A low point for me was _____

_____...

2. ... and I felt _____.

3. A high point for me was _____

_____...

4. ... and I felt _____.

During the past year:

1. A low point for me was _____

_____...

2. ... and I felt _____.

3. A high point for me was _____

_____...

4. ... and I felt _____.

You may be doing check-ins with others every day, once a week, or at some other arranged interval. I would suggest that even if you're meeting with a group once a week, it's still a good idea to write out your check-ins each day for several weeks. You can make copies of the blank check-in form on page 97, or you can write your high points, low points, and feelings in a regular notebook or on the computer. Whatever works for you.

One More Note on Checking In:

If you do check-ins with another person, I would encourage you to resist the urge to debate, argue about, or further explain anything that you or the other person said. One of the best ways to use the check-in process is to be able to express yourself and not have to defend or justify. Practice expressing yourself, listening to the other person, and leaving it at that. There are more tools coming your way for when you need to talk and process through a conflict.

Is It Yours Yet?

Be prepared to answer (either verbally or in writing) the following questions about the check-in process.

1. Name three benefits of doing a check-in.
2. Why is it important to expand your feelings vocabulary?
3. Why is it important to say "I feel" or "I felt" instead of "It made me feel..."?
4. What do words like "good," "bad," "fine," and "okay" have in common?
5. Why is it important to identify both high and low points in each check in?
6. What are the seven main categories of feelings?
7. Why is it better not to debate, argue, or further explain during check-in?

TOOL #3: DEFENSES

Overview:

Learn how you usually defend yourself against stress, fear, and pain. Identify which specific defenses you use, and learn how they affect you and your relationships. Decide which defenses are no longer useful to you, and learn how to let them go and what to do instead.

Getting Started:

Consider the following question: What do you usually do when you don't want to deal with a problem? For example, do you change the subject, argue, hide out in your room, eat chocolate, lie, etc.?

Examples:

When she's stressed, April hibernates in her room, sleeps a lot, eats junk food, holds stress and tension in her neck and shoulders, and is sarcastic a lot of the time.

Your Examples:

Information About Defenses:

Defenses are behaviors or ways of thinking that we use to protect ourselves from being overwhelmed. **Using defenses is normal**, especially when we are very young and don't know what else to do. The problem is that sometimes the defenses become habits, and we keep using them even when they're not working for us anymore. When we use defenses most or all of the time, we end up not dealing with problems, which means that they get bigger and worse, instead of getting resolved.

We use defenses mostly in order to avoid things we don't want to face. Look back at the examples you gave about how you avoid dealing with problems, then take a minute and check off the things you may be trying to avoid.

I probably use defenses to:

[] avoid painful feelings (anger, hurt, fear, guilt, shame, etc.)
[] avoid facing the truth about something that would be painful
[] avoid hurting others
[] avoid the consequences of my actions
[] avoid taking responsibility for my feelings and actions
[] avoid having to change (because change is usually scary)
[] avoid conflict

<u>Basic Defenses</u>:

Here are some basic defenses, and brief definitions of each one. Check the boxes of **all** those you believe you've used at any time in your life, even if you don't use them now:

[] Simple denial: "What problem? There is no problem. Everything's fine."
    (even when there clearly is a problem)
[] Minimizing: "Okay, maybe there's a small, minor problem."
    (when the problem is not small or minor)
[] Repression of feelings or memories:
    "I have no feelings about this problem."
    "I don't remember anything from age 5 to 7."
[] Dissociation: Numbing out or zoning out.

Now check off which specific defenses you believe you've used at some time. This is a long list, so take your time and be honest with yourself:

[] stuffing feelings -- knowing you have feelings but stuffing them away
[] isolating -- separating yourself, either alone or in a crowd
[] silence -- not speaking up or not speaking at all
[] overachieving -- focusing on success and ignoring your feelings
[] perfectionism -- focusing on being perfect and ignoring your feelings
[] depression -- stuffing feelings until you become numb or overwhelmed
[] fake smile -- acting like it's all "fine fine fine" when it isn't
[] anxiety -- tension and the feeling of, "I can't handle this."
[] over-analyzing -- trying to think and solve instead of feel

[] distracting -- changing the subject, acting silly, etc.
[] rescuing -- trying to fix and save others, ignoring your own feelings
[] playing victim -- looking for pity (not support), blaming others
[] control -- trying to control others or to stay in complete control
[] anger -- using anger as a way to keep people away from you
[] hostility -- aiming your anger at others
[] body language -- no eye contact, turning away, eye rolling, etc.
[] putdowns -- negative comments or name-calling
[] sarcasm -- "just joking" but in a mean way
[] gossip -- focusing on others, ignoring your own issues
[] excuses -- justifying and blaming others for your feelings, etc.
[] violence -- fighting, throwing or breaking things, etc.
[] arrogance -- an "I'm above all this" attitude
[] superiority -- an "I'm better than you are" attitude
[] magical thinking -- For example: "My parents have been divorced for fifteen years
       and live hundreds of miles apart, but I still think they'll get back together if I just
       break my leg and they both come to the hospital and see each other again..."
[] lying -- this includes half-truths, leaving out information, etc.
[] blaming -- focusing on others instead of taking responsibility
[] raging -- losing control, screaming & yelling, hurting self or others
[] seductive behavior -- flirting, sexual attention-getting
[] sexual acting out -- using sex the way addicts use drugs -- to numb out
[] running away -- could include avoiding or actually running away
[] self-injury -- cutting, burning, erasing skin, etc.
[] gangs -- affiliation, membership, fighting, criminal activities, etc.
[] stealing -- small scale or large scale
[] vandalism -- tagging, breaking windows, setting fires, etc.
[] prejudice -- race, religion, appearance, clothing, etc.
[] criticizing -- pointing out the negatives, put downs, complaining
[] profanity -- swearing, cussing (distracts from the real feelings)
[] threats -- violence, revenge, threatening to leave, etc.
[] whining -- a form of playing "victim," also distracts
[] needing to be right -- power struggle instead of addressing issues
[] competition -- focusing on winning instead of on resolving issues
[] people pleasing -- going along with others so they'll accept you
[] humor -- jokes, kidding -- the most common form of distraction
[] candy-coated memories -- remembering "perfection" instead of reality
[] overreacting -- another form of distraction
[] obsessing -- thinking and analyzing instead of feeling and releasing
[] black and white thinking -- all or nothing, no middle ground

[] projection -- saying another is angry (hurt, etc.) when really I am
    (for example: the angriest and most hostile person you know keeps saying she
    doesn't know why everyone's so angry all the time)
[] transference -- feeling angry (etc.) at one, but really am at another
    (for example: I'm angry at my dad, but I keep saying how much I can't stand my
    teacher or boss -- who reminds me of my dad)
[] addictions: alcohol, drugs, eating disorders, work, etc.
[] escaping into: TV, sleep, video games, the internet, hobbies, projects
[] physical symptoms: headaches, migraines, stomach aches, ulcers, colds and flu, sore
    muscles, sore throat, rashes, etc.
[] compulsive behavior: excessive shopping, exercising, etc.
[] other:

_____

The Wall of Defenses:

Below is a blank wall. Since defenses can be a way to build a wall against stress and pain, fil
in the bricks with the defenses you use most often. This is the wall you've stood behind
during difficult times. Remember that this isn't necessarily a negative thing. This wall may
have saved your life at some earlier time, but you probably also paid a price for staying
behind it. Now you are learning new tools to address issues, so you can step out from
behind the wall and still be safe.

Now look back at the defenses checklist and write down the following:

1. How many defenses you checked: _____

    (This is **not** an indicator of how "messed up" or unhealthy you are. I see it as an indicator of how much stress you've had to deal with!)

2. The top five defenses you currently use:

3. The top five defenses you used in the past, but not currently:

4. The one defense that currently causes you the most problems:

5. The one defense that you know you don't want to give up yet:

The <u>Problem With Defenses</u>:

As I said earlier, defenses themselves are not a negative thing, and they may have been life-saving at one time. Unfortunately, with continued use, most of them come with a big price tag or other consequences.

Example: Jennifer, a high school English teacher, paid a big price tag for being sarcastic (and crossing the line between funny and mean) because without meaning to, she pushed people away, or they became cautious around her. Early in her teaching career, a student pointed out to her that he didn't want to talk or write about personal issues in her English class, because he didn't know what she might say. He was very nice about it, but she was shocked -- she had always encouraged students to write about real things in their lives, and here was this young man she really liked and admired, telling her that he didn't feel safe around her.

They had that conversation on the day before school ended. The following year (and ever since), Jennifer has made a point of still kidding around with students, but never crossing the line between funny and mean. She had developed the habit of sarcasm to defend against things happening in her house as she was growing up, but she hadn't realized how it was affecting the people around her in her adult life. She's still grateful to that student for pointing that out to her.

Your Turn

Please list any five of your defenses below (past or current), and identify consequences that have surfaced for you as a result of using them:

Another example: Defense: People-pleasing
Consequence: I don't stand up for myself so people don't know who I am or what I feel.

1. Defense: _____

   Consequence: _____

2. Defense: _____

   Consequence: _____

3. Defense: _____

   Consequence: _____

4. Defense: _____

   Consequence: _____

5. Defense: _____

   Consequence: _____

Now What?

The next step is figuring out what to do instead of using the defenses. Since defenses are ways to avoid stress and conflict, what usually works is to identify what would be the most direct way to address the issue instead.

For instance, if sarcasm is one of your defenses, one way to be more direct about it is to make a clear "I" statement about how you really feel. If lying is one of your defenses, one way to be more direct is to tell the whole truth to someone, even if you just write it down in a journal at first. If perfectionism is one of your defenses, you can remind yourself that you're human, perfectly imperfect, and that it's okay to make mistakes. You can even write that on a Post-it note and stick it on your bathroom mirror.

Now, list your top five current defenses, and for each one, identify one or more ways to address the issue directly:

Example: Defense: People pleasing
             Address Directly By: Thinking about what I really want, and speaking up.

1. Defense: _____

   Address Directly By: _____

   _____

2. Defense: _____

   Address Directly By: _____

   _____

3. Defense: _____

   Address Directly By: _____

   _____

4. Defense: _____

   Address Directly By: _____

   _____

5. Defense: _____

   Address Directly By: _____

   _____

Closure/Practice:

Letting go of defenses takes time, practice, and persistence. I would recommend that you choose one defense to work on releasing, be aware of it for the next few weeks, and practice dealing directly with it instead. Which defense will you work on letting go of first?

_____

Is It Yours Yet?

Be prepared to answer (either verbally or in writing) the following questions about defenses.

1. What are defenses, and why do we use them?
2. If defenses are normal, why do we need to become aware of them?
3. When can using defenses become a problem?
4. Give three examples of things people avoid by using defenses.
5. Give five examples of specific defenses.
6. Why are a set of defenses called a wall?
7. What can we learn to do instead of using defenses?

TOOL #4: WHAT'S UNDER ANGER:

Overview:

Learn how anger, hurt, fear, and other feelings go together, and how to sort out all your feelings about a situation, identify your needs, take steps toward resolving the situation, and take care of yourself no matter what.

Getting Started:

Think of a situation in your life (preferably a current situation, but if not, a significant one from the past) that you are either really angry about, or that you have lots of frustration and other feelings about.

My Example:

I'm going to use one from a former client (with her permission, and a different name): Brooke was 14 at the time, and the situation was that she rarely got to spend time with her father. He was a doctor who spent most of his days working, and she felt hurt, left out, and angry, among other things.

Your Situation:

We'll come back to this situation later. First, some information to help you use the "What's Under Anger" tool.

The Basics of Working With Feelings:

In order to work with your feelings effectively, it's important to understand more about what they are, why we have them, and how they work. There are various viewpoints out there about the system of human emotions. After learning many different theories, and then working with hundreds of people in one setting or another over a period of years, this is the viewpoint that works for me:

The word emotion (e-motion) stands for energy in motion. When our emotions are in good working order, they do two things. **First, they alert us** that something important is happening. If we're in the woods and a bear shows up and starts chasing us, fear kicks in, the adrenaline races through our bodies, and sends us the signal to run. If we respond quickly (in this case, run, climb a tree, or whatever), and the danger passes, then the feelings do their second function, which is to **move through our bodies and out**. At first we shake, breathe more heavily, and our hearts pound, and then we calm down, relax more, and our systems return to normal.

All of the basic human emotions, except one, which we'll come back to, work this way when the system is balanced. The feeling first alerts us to something important, and then it moves through our bodies and out. It's doing its job, and then when the job is done, it returns the system to normal. All feelings can be expressed (moved through the system) in either productive or unproductive ways. Here's a breakdown of some of the main feelings and how they commonly operate:

-- Anger usually alerts us that something feels unfair or out of line. We move it through our systems with physical activity, use of the big muscles in our arms and back (exercising, fighting, throwing), or through verbal expression (talking or yelling).

-- Hurt usually alerts us that we've lost something important. We move it most effectively through our systems with tears, and through talking with others.

-- Fear alerts us that our safety is threatened. We move it through our system with adrenaline, and express it with physical activity (like running), or verbal expression (talking or screaming).

-- Guilt alerts us that we're acting outside of our own "rules" or values (not someone else's; that's more likely to produce fear of consequences than guilt). We move it through our systems by correcting our behavior or through verbal expression (talking, "confessing," apologizing).

-- Happiness or joy alerts us that we're aligned or being true to ourselves. It's harder to define than some of the other feelings, but we certainly know it when we feel it. We express it physically (jumping up and down, hugging someone) or verbally (enthusiastic yelling, talking), and sometimes by crying when we're deeply touched by something.

Some Q & A About Feelings:

The following are some basic questions about feelings. The answers are on the following page, so the reason for including the questions here is basically to get you thinking in depth about this topic. See what you can come up with regarding the following:

1. What two feelings are always underneath anger, even if we are not aware of them?

2. Why do some people cover up other feelings with anger?

3. Why is it important to look underneath anger for the other feelings?

4. What is the difference between guilt and shame?

5. What is the only unproductive emotion? Why is it unproductive?

6. What are some of the things that happen if people stuff feelings instead of expressing them? List at least five.

7. Rage is made up of four feelings. What are they?

8. What uncomfortable feeling or feelings do you feel the most often? How do you usually handle that feeling? What would be the healthiest way to handle it?

Feelings Q & A -- Answers:

1. What two feelings are always underneath anger, even if we are not aware of them?

   Hurt and fear.

   I can't tell you how many hundreds of times I've had people come into my office, boiling mad, and if I let them talk about it without interruption and without trying to fix it for them, they'll talk and rant for awhile, and then they'll take a breath, and the sadness will just pour out. Then they'll talk (and maybe cry) for awhile, and again, if I just let them do it, and don't get in their way, they'll take another breath, and out will come this small voice, and they'll start talking about fears. This happens naturally, without any prompting from me.

   For instance, if someone tells me that a parent or partner makes rude and critical remarks for no apparent reason, the anger is that the comments seem unfair and uncalled for. The hurt is that the person wants support and encouragement from the parent or partner and isn't getting it, and the fear is that it may always be this way, or get worse. This is a generic example, but the dynamics are the same for many situations.

   Sometimes we aren't connected to the hurt or fear (or even to the anger). When I'm talking with someone who only feels one or two of the feelings, I might offer an idea or a possibility, but I don't tell people how they feel. With support, most people are able to identify their own underlying feelings.

2. Why do some people cover up other feelings with anger?

   Because anger is more acceptable in our society -- expressing anger looks "tough" or "strong." Also, many people feel too vulnerable or "weak" when they express hurt and fear.

3. Why is it important to look underneath anger for the other feelings?

Because if we don't, we stay stuck in anger and can't move forward or resolve conflicts effectively. If we're stuck in anger, we may feel powerful (falsely), but nothing is really getting addressed or resolved.

4. What is the difference between guilt and shame?

Guilt and shame are related, but they aren't the same thing. Guilt is about what we do or don't do -- it's about behavior. Shame is deeper -- it's about who we are as human beings.

If we fail an important test and feel **guilty**, we think: "I know I could have done better on that if I'd studied more. Next time I'll do better." If we fail that same test and feel **shame**, we think, "I'm just too stupid to learn this," or maybe, "I'm hopeless and I might as well quit school right now."

5. What is the only unproductive emotion? Why is it unproductive?

This is a touchy question, because of the implication that shame is "unhealthy." It has been taught for many years it's been taught that there are no unhealthy feelings, that all feelings are healthy and it's what you do with them that counts. This is why I use the word "unproductive" instead of unhealthy. As you read on, I hope my reasoning will be clear.

The difference between shame and other feelings is that shame doesn't move. Anger moves, guilt moves, sadness moves, etc., but when we're feeling shame, we feel "stuck." Shame says that who we are as human beings is not good enough. If we feel "stupid," "worthless," "ugly," etc., we believe that's who we are and that's the way it is.

There are also therapists and other mental health professionals out there who divide the concept of shame into two categories, healthy shame and toxic shame. They define toxic shame the way I just described it, as not feeling good enough, etc. They define healthy shame as "the awareness of your imperfections and limits as a human being." Personally, I'd rather call that "acceptance of human limitations" and leave it at that. I don't think that's shame. I understand the connection, but I think they're two different things.

6. What are some of the things that happen if people stuff feelings instead of expressing them? List at least five.

   Physical illness, aches and pains, raging, sleep disturbance, relationship problems, addictions and compulsions, suicide attempts, problems with authority, etc.

7. Rage is made up of four feelings. What are they?

   Anger, hurt, fear, and shame. We'll come back to that one later, but it's included here as food for thought.

8. What uncomfortable feeling or feelings do you feel the most often? How do you usually handle that feeling? What would be the healthiest way to handle it?

   Of course, answers to this will vary. And if you found that you weren't sure of the healthiest way to handle uncomfortable feelings, that will probably change as you work with these tools.

Using the "What's Under Anger" Tool:

"What's Under Anger" is a ten-step process, which you can either write down or talk through with someone, or both. The following is some background information to help you use this tool most effectively:

You can use this process in the following situations:

-- When you feel stuck in anger.
-- When you feel overwhelmed by lots of different feelings.
-- When you find yourself obsessing about a problem.
-- When you feel confused and don't know what to do.
-- When you can't find someone to talk to about your feelings.
-- When you don't know where to start in problem solving.

This process will help you:

-- sort out the situation and understand it more clearly.
-- identify your feelings and needs.
-- work through and express feelings.

-- get "un-stuck" and move forward.
-- let go of a problem that keeps spinning around in your head.
-- take responsibility for your part in a problem.
-- hold other people accountable for their parts in a problem.
-- figure out what steps to take in order to take care of yourself.

As you already know, ANGER, HURT, and FEAR always go together, even if you are only feeling one of them. Picture three layers of feelings, with anger at the top, a layer of hurt underneath, and a layer of fear at the bottom. Anger is usually the easiest to feel and express, and once you work through the anger, the hurt rises to the top and can also be expressed. Then the fear rises to the top, and you can work through it too.

WISHES, WANTS, and NEEDS go together, and each one is important for its own reason. Wishes are unlimited, and it doesn't matter if you wish for something impossible, as long as you don't stay "stuck" in that impossible wish. Wants are things that are important to you and add to your happiness, but that you could live without. Needs are things important to your survival or your health (physical or emotional).

ACCEPTANCE and UNDERSTANDING go together. Acceptance can be the hardest part of this process, but it helps you move on. Sometimes you can accept responsibility for your part in a problem. Sometimes you can accept who or what you can't change. Sometimes you can simply accept that something happened, even though you wish it hadn't. Understanding can also help you move on. You can understand why something happened or why someone did something hurtful, and you still have the right to all your feelings.

TAKING CARE OF YOURSELF IN THE SITUATION is absolutely necessary, and sometimes it's the only thing you can do. Even if you can't change what happened or what another person is doing, you can find ways to survive the problem and be good to yourself. Taking this step is the most important way to get "un-stuck" and move forward.

Whenever possible, share what you wrote with someone you trust.

Here's a great example of the use of this format from Brooke, the client I mentioned earlier. Using this process was a turning point for her, and I'll talk about why, but first, her example:

WHAT'S UNDER ANGER

1. **The situation is...**   *that my dad works all the time and I never see him. Even when he is home, he spends all his time with my brother, and not with me.*

2. **I'm angry because...**   *he makes excuses. I'm also angry because he promises to spend time with me and then never does -- there's always some reason.*

3. **I'm hurt because...**   *I feel left out, and it feels like he loves my brother more than he loves me. I'm also hurt because I miss him. We used to spend time together.*

4. **My fear is...**   *that he doesn't really love me, and that I might lose him.*

5. **I wish...**   *he didn't work so much. I wish I was little again so he would still pay attention to me. I wish it was the way it used to be.*

6. **I want...**   *him to keep his promises. I want him to understand how I feel.*

7. **I need...**   *A FATHER.*

8. **I accept...**   *that he works long hours. I accept that I can't change him or make him keep his promises. He's the only one who can change himself.*

9. **I understand...**   *that he works long hours because he wants the extra money. He grew up poor and wants a better life for us. (I'd still rather have him than the money.)*

10. **To take care of myself in this situation, I'm going to...**   *tell him (or my mom, or someone I trust) about my anger, hurt, and fear. I'm also going to spend some weekends with my friends instead of sitting around waiting for him and being hurt when he cancels or doesn't show up. And when I do have plans with him, I'll have a back-up plan with a friend so I'm never left just sitting there again.*

Until she used this process to sort things out, Brooke was only aware of her anger. She hadn't acknowledged even to herself how hurt she felt, what her fears were, or that she felt like she didn't have a father. She also didn't know how to answer #10, and ended up needing feedback from other members of the group she was in (supportive feedback is the next tool you'll learn). Someone else suggested the part about having a back-up plan with friends, and she said she would never have thought of that on her own.

Once she sorted out her feelings, she was able to talk about the situation with her parents for the first time. They made some changes as a family, and her father gained a real understanding about what was happening with his daughter -- he hadn't known how strongly she felt about his long hours at work, because she'd never really talked about it before.

Your Turn:

Use the What's Under Anger steps to process the sample situation you wrote at the beginning of this chapter, or another situation you can think of that you have lots of feelings about, and see what you come up with.

WHAT'S UNDER ANGER

1. The situation is...

2. I'm angry because...

3. I'm hurt because...

4. My fear is...

5. I wish...

6. I want...

7. I need...

8. I accept...

9. I understand...

10. To take care of myself in this situation, I'm going to...

Now What?

First, see if you can find someone to share this with -- a parent, teacher, counselor, or other trusted adult, a support group, or a friend your own age. Let the person or people know that you don't need anyone to fix it for you, just to listen. When you're going to share a "What's Under Anger" sheet with someone, ask if they will please just listen without interruption, and if someone is sharing feelings with you, I would encourage you to give that person the same courtesy.

Second, do whatever you said you were going to do in #10 in order to take care of yourself, as long as it harms no one (including you). When you get to the final tool in this workbook, you'll find a whole list of ways to take care of yourself in stressful situations.

Third, use this format whenever you need to sort things out or express lots of feelings about a situation. Make copies of the blank worksheet from page 98, and keep them handy, or just use the ten statements and write in your journal, on the computer, etc. Another thing I would encourage is that you date and keep each one you write. This is another great form of journaling, and you can mark your progress as you go along.

Fourth, go to the next tool -- supportive feedback -- and learn how to respond when someone wants to sort out situations or express feelings with you. You can also teach the supportive feedback process to important people in your life so they can offer it to you when you need it.

Is It Yours Yet?

Be prepared to answer (either verbally or in writing) the following questions about the What's Under Anger process.

1. What does the word "emotion" stand for?
2. What are the two things our emotions do for us when our systems are in balance?
3. What two feelings are always underneath anger?
4. What is the difference between guilt and shame?
5. How is shame different from other emotions?
6. Name three things that the What's Under Anger process can help us do.
7. What is the difference between wishes, wants, and needs?
8. Why is step 10 (taking care of yourself in the situation) so important?

TOOL #5: SUPPORTIVE FEEDBACK

Overview:

Learn to offer support to someone else without giving advice or trying to fix the situation. Practice your listening skills, use your "I" statements again, and learn to validate what the other person is feeling -- a far more useful and helpful skill than having all the answers.

Getting Started:

Think of a time you remember trying to talk with someone, telling that person how you felt or what your frustrations were, but you found yourself getting even more frustrated because the person didn't know how to respond to you.

Example:

Jeff has a friend who believes she's a great listener, but when he tries to talk to her about something serious in his life, she keeps interrupting him, telling him she knows exactly how he feels, and then interrupts him some more. Every time he tries to get back to his feelings, she cuts him off, and he leaves the conversation more frustrated than he was in the first place.

Your Example:

About Supportive Feedback:

You can use this information to give healthy, supportive feedback when someone is sharing feelings or talking about issues. You may also want to give this information to others and teach them how to give you supportive feedback.

When someone wants to talk, but the listeners don't know how to respond, here are some of the things people do:

1. They give advice, try to "fix" things, or tell you what you "should" do.

2. They interrupt or distract with questions, try to show you that they understand, but really make it more difficult for you to talk.

3. They try to top your story: "I know how you feel. I remember the time when I..."

4. They invalidate your feelings: "It's not that bad." "Don't worry about it." "There's nothing to be afraid of." "Cheer up." "Don't cry." "Smile." "Everything will be fine."

5. They tell you how you feel or how you should feel, or that they know exactly how you feel, even when they don't.

-- Which one of the above types of unproductive feedback bothers you the most when you hear it?

-- Which one (or more) do you know you've done at one time or another?

Most of us who give these responses mean well -- we just haven't learned a more productive way to give feedback. Here's a feedback format that works better and is much more supportive:

1. Show the person you were really listening by not interrupting or asking any questions as they talk. **Ask if the person is open to hearing feedback**, then summarize briefly what the person was saying.

   You say: "I heard you say..."

2. Without telling the person what he or she feels, state what feelings you believe you saw, heard, or sensed. This is validating for the other person without violating any boundaries.

You say: "The feelings I saw (heard/sensed) were..."

3. Give encouragement and support, rather than advice, and tell the person how you identify with the situation, if you do. You can use one of these or more than one, in the order given. Remember not to use "shoulds."

You say: "I encourage you to..."   AND/OR
"I support you in..."   AND/OR

"I can identify because..."

This process will feel awkward at first, and you don't need to use it all the time, just when someone is sharing something difficult or significant. It's a formal process, but it works well because when someone gives us feedback, 1) we know they've really heard what we said, 2) we know we've expressed our feelings clearly, 3) we have some ideas or suggestions to try, and 4) we know that we're not the only one who feels these feelings -- we're not weird and we're not alone.

Examples:

Let's say that you were in the group where Brooke read her "What's Under Anger" worksheet, and you were chosen to give her supportive feedback. Here are two examples, a short version and a more detailed version. If you hadn't had much practice with this process, you might say:

"Brooke, can I offer you some feedback? "If she said yes, you might say, "**I heard you say** that your dad works a lot and doesn't spend time with you the way he used to. **The feelings I heard** were sadness and fear. **I encourage you to** let your dad know how you feel, and **I support you in** having back-up plans with your friends. **I can identify because** I used to have a closer relationship with my dad than I do now, and I miss him."

You could also pick another way to identify with her, such as, "**I can identify because** I hate the feeling of sitting around waiting for someone who's late." You don't have to have experienced the exact same situation, just one where you had similar feelings. With practice, this is easier to do.

If you'd had practice with the feedback format, you could give more detailed feedback, such as the following:

"Brooke, can I offer you some feedback?

"**I heard you say** that your dad works all the time and you don't get to see him. I heard that he promises to meet you at certain times, but doesn't show up, and you're left waiting there. I heard that he spends more time with your brother than with you, and that you're feeling like you don't have a father, and that you're afraid that he loves your brother more than he does you.

"**The feelings I heard** were hurt, sadness, fear, and shame. The biggest fear I heard was that you might lose your relationship with your dad.

"**I encourage you to** talk to your parents about this so they both know what's going on and how hurt you feel. I especially encourage you to talk with your dad, in case he just doesn't get it and has no idea.

"**I support you in** making back-up plans with your friends, and I support you in talking about this with the group instead of keeping it to yourself.

"**I can identify because** there was a time when I was younger that I was a lot closer to my dad than I am now, and I miss that. I can also identify because I don't like the feeling of having promises broken, and sitting around waiting for someone who's late all the time."

With practice, you'll be able to remember a lot more of what the other person said, and to give more detailed feedback.

More Things to Keep In Mind:

When you're learning and practicing this process, it's important that a person's feedback not be interrupted with questions or corrections. If someone is giving you feedback that you disagree with (which will sometimes happen), you can still listen, and then choose on your own whether to use particular ideas or not. The most appropriate response when someone gives you feedback is to listen silently until they're finished, and then say, "Thank you."

Practice:

Here's a sample of someone sharing feelings about a situation, but in a less organized way than the "What's Under Anger" sheet. Read through it, and then fill in the feedback you would give that person:

"I'm so tired of my friend borrowing things from me and not returning them, I could just scream. She's borrowed a lot of money from me, borrowed clothes, and she has five of my CDs that I don't think I'm ever going to see again. Whenever I bring it up, she just says, "Oops -- sorry about that," and tells me she'll return things to me the next day, and then she doesn't. If I call her, she doesn't answer her phone, and I've just about had it with this friendship. We've known each other a long time, and I know she's been stressed out lately, but I just can't take it anymore. This has been going on for months. I'm about ready to get my stuff back from her and tell her to get out of my life."

Your Feedback:

1. I heard you say...

2. The feelings I heard (saw, sensed) were...

3. I encourage you to...

4. I support you in...

5. I can identify because...

Now What?

Now you need practice. If you're working with a friend, counselor, or group, ask for examples of "What's Under Anger" or just share feelings about a situation, and practice giving feedback. You don't particularly need to write it down, just follow the format and speak your feedback to the other person.

Also, you may want to share your earlier "What's Under Anger" sheet and ask for supportive feedback from someone else. If you're doing this workbook on your own, I would encourage you to find at least one person willing to learn the feedback process, so you can practice with each other.

In your practice, remember your "I" statements. All the beginning statements in the feedback process are already "I" statements, but stick to them as closely as you can. If you start saying, "You're feeling," instead of "The feelings I heard were," or saying "You need to" or "You should" instead of, "I encourage you to," the tone of the conversation will change dramatically.

You can also use this format when you're in conflict with someone. One person shares feelings, and the other gives **only** supportive feedback. Then the second person shares feelings, and the first gives **only** supportive feedback. (NOTE: If you're angry with each other, you may want to just do the first two steps of the process. Also, make sure you leave out the word "but," as in, "I heard you say _____, BUT," or "The feelings I heard were _____, BUT"... That word used in that way can kill a great conversation.) If there's still a lot of tension, the two of you can set a time-out from the topic of the conflict, and come back to it later. Sometimes just knowing that your words and your feelings are being heard and validated makes all the difference.

<u>Is It Yours Yet?</u>

Be prepared to answer (either verbally or in writing) the following questions about supportive feedback.

1. Name three less-than-helpful things listeners do when they don't know how to respond with supportive feedback.
2. List the five steps of supportive feedback.
3. Why is it important to ask, "Can I offer you some feedback?" before beginning?
4. What word do we especially need to avoid when giving encouragement and support?
5. Name four benefits of having someone give us supportive feedback.
6. How can we say, "I can identify..." if we haven't been in the same situation as the person we're giving feedback to?
7. What is an appropriate response when someone gives us feedback we disagree with?

TOOL #6: THE RAGE BOMB

(Note: This activity is adapted from information provided by The Meadows, in Wickenburg, AZ)

Overview:

Learn how anger and rage are different, and what all the components of rage are. Identify your own rage triggers and behaviors, and learn how to diffuse the bomb before it explodes.

Getting Started:

Think of a time that you can remember being so angry that you either lost control of your behavior (yelling, screaming, hitting, throwing, etc.) or sat there boiling internally but kept quiet because you knew that if you did open your mouth, you'd be in big trouble. If you honestly can't think of a time you did this or felt like this, think of a time you saw someone else do it.

My Example:

A personal example: I'll go into more detail on this later in this section, but the bottom line is that one night when I was 17, I was so furious with my parents that I got going with a baseball bat in the basement, and I hardly even remember the details.

Your Example:

A Rage Survey:

Before we get into the background and components of rage, please take a few minutes to do the following checklist. All these behaviors, **done when you're angry**, qualify as acts of rage. Mark the box of each one you've ever done, even if it was years or decades ago:

ACTS OF RAGE

Physical:

[] Hitting walls or objects
[] hitting, punching, or slapping someone
[] fist fighting
[] pushing, shoving, or kicking someone
[] breaking things
[] throwing things
[] knocking over furniture
[] slamming doors, cabinets, etc.
[] tearing apart a room
[] destroying things
[] attacks involving weapons
[] aggression toward animals: teasing, hitting, kicking, or killing them

Emotional:

[] yelling or screaming at someone
[] name calling or profanity directed at someone
[] threatening
[] felony fantasies (imagining doing horrible things to someone)

Symbolic:

[] fire setting (there's a huge correlation between rage and fire setting)
[] vandalism
[] theft

Turning Rage Inward:

[] cutting or burning yourself
[] cutting or shaving off your hair (in anger, not just trimming your bangs)
[] picking at scabs or sores on a regular basis
[] binge eating, purging, or self-starvation (eating disorder behaviors)
[] suicide attempts

[] others: _____

1. List the four or five acts of rage that you currently do the most often.

2. List the four or five acts of rage that you've done in the past, but you rarely or never do now.

About Rage:

Many people believe that rage is just anger with the volume turned up, but there's more to it than that. You've already learned that hurt and fear are always under anger, and rage adds another feeling to the mix -- **shame**. Along with feeling "stupid" or "worthless" when we feel shame, the other most common experience is feeling **powerless**. For example, if someone is making fun of us in front of a group and everyone is laughing, we not only feel hurt, belittled, etc., we also feel powerless because we can't make the person stop teasing us, and we can't stop everyone from laughing. The feeling of powerlessness on some level (along with anger, hurt, and fear) is the most common trigger for rage.

Another difference between anger and rage is that **anger is a feeling** , but **rage is a behavior** -- it's the out-of-control response to having anger, hurt, fear, and shame stuffed inside you until there's no more room to contain it.

Some people build up to rage slowly. It takes them a long time to get to the point of losing control and raging. Other people seem to rage about every little thing. When that happens, chances are that the person has been carrying around a lot of painful feelings for quite awhile, and doesn't know what to do with them. So that person has built a sort of container for all the feelings and tried to keep them shut away. The problem with doing that is that all those containers eventually leak, and there's only so much room inside any one person for emotional containers. Emotions are designed to be expressed, and one way or another, they always come out.

Diffusing Rage:

The good news is that rage can be diffused and expressed, and the process is not all that complicated. When I first saw this process, I thought it was a nice theory, but I doubted that it would really work, because it seemed so simple. I had lots of rage, and didn't see how this process could make any significant difference. Fortunately, I was wrong. Since I've learned and used the process, I've also taught it to a lot of people who initially thought the same thing I did, and it's worked for them too.

The rage bomb can be used in two ways. The first is to look at a time you raged in the past, and sort out the feelings you were having **just before** (not after) you lost control and raged. This strongly reduces the likelihood of you raging again about the same situation or issue. The second way is to look at a situation you feel like raging about now, but would like to prevent. If you can identify the anger, hurt, fear, and shame you're feeling now, the chances of you losing control and raging are also dramatically reduced.

The bottom line is that if you can identify the separate feelings that make up rage, you are separating the components and diffusing the bomb so it can't explode. The Rage Bomb is very much a tool of empowerment. If you use it consistently, you will see a reduction in your raging behaviors.

<u>My Example:</u>

Here's an example of my own to illustrate the process. I grew up in a tense alcoholic household. I was the only child, and I didn't talk much about what was happening with anyone, partly because I didn't think they'd believe me. My parents put on a great public face, and I wasn't as good at that as they were, so I had occasional troubles at school (particularly in 8th grade) with my attitude and my mouth.

By the time I was 17, I had myself under control pretty well, did well in school, etc. But one night, my parents were getting ready to go out somewhere, and were getting dressed up and shoe-shined, and they were also sort of sniping at each other verbally. Then they went to the front door, turned to me, smiled, and said very sweetly, "We'll see you later -- have a nice night!" or something equally fake.

The next thing I remember was standing in the basement with a baseball bat in my hand, slamming it repeatedly into one of those iron support poles that hold up the house. I did it for a long time, until my arms got numb, then I dropped the bat and sat on the edge of my bed, waiting for the men with the straitjackets to come and take me away. I think I'd been building up that rage for about six years.

On the following page is a sample of the rage worksheet, based on that example:

"RAGE BOMB" WORKSHEET -- Diffusing the Bomb

1. What was the situation you raged about?

My parents were tense and sniping at each other, then put on their fake smiles and went out the door, the same way they've done for my whole life.

2. What act of rage did you do?

I took a baseball bat and smashed it repeatedly against a pole in our basement for about ten minutes, until I couldn't do it anymore.

3. Fill in the following statements:

I felt **angry** because: *It was all such a lie. My parents acted sweet and wonderful in public, but at home no one ever really talked to each other.*

I felt **hurt** because: *It was such a lonely and miserable place to be. I spent most of my time alone in my room, doing homework and writing.*

I felt **fear** because: *I was afraid every family was like this, and no one would admit it. I was afraid I'd grow up and be just like my parents. I was afraid that if I told anyone what it was like in my house, no one would believe me.*

I felt **shame/powerless** because: *There was nothing I could do about it -- I was powerless over what people thought of me and my family. I also felt shame because my 8th grade English teacher once said, "What's wrong with Susan anyway? She has such a nice family!"*

4. What could you do in the future to take care of yourself instead of raging?

*Talk to someone I trust -- tell **someone** what was going on and how I felt. I could also (and did) write journal entries almost every day.*

<u>Your Turn</u>:

"RAGE BOMB" WORKSHEET -- Diffusing the Bomb

1. What was the situation you raged about?

2. What act of rage did you do?

3. Fill in the following statements:

   I felt **angry** because:

   I felt **hurt** because:

   I felt **fear** because:

   I felt **shame/powerless** because:

4. What could you do in the future to take care of yourself instead of raging?

Part 2: RAGE PREVENTION WORKSHEET

You can use this version in a situation where you **feel like raging**, but have not done it yet. Here's an example:

1. What is the situation that you feel like raging about?

My boss keeps making comments about how women are lazy, dumb, and too emotional, and then he looks right at me.

2. What do you feel like doing, that you have to hold yourself back from?

Honestly, I feel like wrapping the phone cord around his neck so tight that even the Jaws of Life couldn't get him out!

3. Fill in the following statements:

I'm **angry** because: *What he's doing is rude and unprofessional.*

I'm **hurt** because: *He's insulting me and not giving me credit for all the hard work I do, and how well I do it.*

My **fear** is: *That if I say anything, I'll lose my job, and that other people at work will take on the same attitude that he models.*

I feel **shame/powerless** because: *The things he says are belittling, and I feel powerless because I can't stand up for myself without risking my job. It's a great job -- I just can't stand him!*

4. What is one healthy way you can take care of yourself instead of raging?

I can vent my feelings somewhere else, with a safe person who doesn't work there. I can also file a formal grievance against him if this continues. If that doesn't help, I can look for another job.

On the following page, fill in your example of a situation you feel like raging about, but would like to prevent:

RAGE PREVENTION WORKSHEET

1. What is the situation that you feel like raging about?

2. What do you feel like doing, that you have to hold yourself back from?

3. Fill in the following statements:

I'm **angry** because:

I'm **hurt** because:

My **fear** is:

I feel **shame/powerless** because:

4. What is one healthy way you can take care of yourself instead of raging?

Now What?

Now, find someone to share your worksheets with, preferably someone who can give you supportive feedback about your experiences.

I would also suggest that you keep copies of your rage worksheets, so you can have a record of your progress, and to look for patterns so you can know more specifically what areas you need to work on. There are blank copies of the worksheets on pages 99-100.

Diffusing rage can take a lot of practice -- it took a lot to get those of us who rage to the explosion point, and it takes some work to clear out all the feelings we've stuffed over the years. Keep working at it -- don't give up!

Is It Yours Yet?

Be prepared to answer (either verbally or in writing) the following questions about rage and the rage bomb.

1. Along with anger, hurt, and fear, what other feeling(s) contribute to rage?
2. How are anger and rage different from each other?
3. What are the four categories of acts of rage?
4. How does using the rage bomb worksheet diffuse rage?
5. How can using the rage bomb make any difference after we've already raged about something?

TOOL # 7: COMMUNICATION STYLES

Overview:

Learn the difference between aggressive, passive, passive-aggressive and assertive behaviors and communication styles. Identify which styles you typically use, the pros and cons of each style, the benefits for you of becoming more assertive, and how to get there.

Background Information:

There are four basic communications styles, and each one has its benefits and consequences. Read the following section and answer the questions as they apply to you.

1. What does it mean to be **aggressive**?

   -- being stuck in anger, arguing, blaming, yelling
   -- making "you" statements, violating boundaries
   -- not respecting others' feelings
   -- being pushy, demanding, taking from others
   -- being intimidating, loud, raging, not listening
   -- trying to solve things through violence or destruction
   -- going after what you want, regardless of the cost to self or others

2. What "**benefits**" can we appear to get from being aggressive?

   -- getting our way   -- not feeling vulnerable
   -- feeling powerful   -- not having to listen
   -- feeling in control   -- getting away with things
   -- feeling invincible

3. What are the **negative consequences** of being aggressive?

   -- pushing people away   -- financial consequences for damage
   -- not trusted by others   -- being feared, not respected
   -- legal consequences   -- stuck in anger, can't move on

4. In what ways have you been **aggressive**? What have been the consequences?

Example: Kim once went along with some teasing that her friends were doing to another girl in their class (6th grade). At one point the girl said, "Kim, if you call me that one more time, I'm going to punch you in the mouth." At a friend's encouragement, Kim did it again, and the other girl put her down on the playground asphalt with one punch.

Kim's consequences were A) getting face-planted on the asphalt, and B) feeling guilty later because that girl had never done anything to her in the first place.

Your example and consequences:

5. What does it mean to be **passive**?

-- avoiding conflict   -- agreeing just to keep the peace
-- smiling a lot   -- saying what others want to hear
-- not showing anger   -- being a doormat
-- denying having needs   -- always putting others first
-- being afraid of anger   -- backing down easily
-- apologizing when others are abusive

6. What "**benefits**" can we appear to get through being passive?

-- having fewer conflicts   -- not taking many risks
-- being seen as "nice"   -- feeling "safe" (falsely)
-- not getting in trouble

7. What are the **negative consequences** of being passive?

-- needs don't get met   -- stuck in fear, can't take action
-- getting dumped on   -- opinions aren't respected
-- getting ignored   -- always being expected to agree

-- being lonely   -- being fake or dishonest
-- all the negative consequences of stuffing feelings (many!)

8. In what ways have you been **passive**? What have been the consequences?

Example: For most of his teenage years and into early adulthood, Mark basically avoided his parents, and didn't tell them how he felt about things, or what he wanted or needed. It was just easier that way, and Mark also avoided the problems and conflicts his parents had.

His consequences were A) His parents didn't really know him at all, B) They had no connection or closeness, and C) When Mark finally did start speaking up about things, years later, his parents were uncomfortable and saw him as a troublemaker in the family.

Your example and consequences:

9. What does it mean to be **passive-aggressive**?

     -- pretending to be passive, but then being aggressive in a sneaky way
     -- getting even without getting caught
     -- closed or avoidant body language
     -- making mean comments, then saying, "Just kidding"
     -- rolling your eyes (then denying having done it)
     -- telling half-truths   -- being two-faced
     -- giving dirty looks   -- making faces behind people's backs
     -- acting innocent   -- being sarcastic

10. What "**benefits**" can we appear to get from being passive-aggressive?

     -- feeling powerful, in control, and "better than"
     -- sometimes having an audience, making people laugh
     -- taking fewer risks than being directly aggressive
     -- thinking we're getting away with things

11. What are the **negative consequences** of being passive-aggressive?

  -- pushing people away
  -- people not feeling safe with us or trusting us
  -- staying stuck in anger, not processing other feelings
  -- focusing on getting even instead of making things better
  -- no-win situation (feels like winning; nothing gets solved)
  -- keeping the conflict going, no resolution

12. In what ways have you been **passive-aggressive**? What have been the consequences?

Example: Michelle got into trouble in a relationship she was in. Her boyfriend would make critical remarks, and when he wasn't looking, Michelle would salute him behind his back. Needless to say, she eventually got caught.

The consequences were that A) It didn't help in any way to resolve the conflicts they were having, and B) He trusted her even less after that.

Your example and consequences:

13. What does it mean to be **assertive**?

  -- using "I" statements   -- expressing feelings directly
  -- no mind games   -- expressing wants and needs directly
  -- no blaming   -- accepting natural consequences
  -- no shaming   -- setting healthy boundaries
  -- listening to others   -- speaking up for ourselves
  -- expressing opinions   -- telling the whole truth
  -- respecting self   -- treating others with respect
  -- taking responsibility for our own thoughts, feelings, and behaviors

14. What are the **negative consequences** of being assertive?

   -- having some people disagree with us
   -- recognizing that we can't change other people
   -- having to deal with consequences of our actions
   -- having some people not be assertive in return
   -- feeling feelings (which sometimes means feeling pain)
   -- not always getting what we asked for
   -- having some people feel threatened by our assertiveness

15. What **benefits** do we get from being assertive?
   -- having many people respect us for our assertiveness
   -- being free from the burden of trying to change people
   -- getting the rewards of our healthy actions
   -- having many people be assertive in return
   -- feeling feelings (which sometimes means feeling happiness)
   -- often getting what we ask for
   -- honesty means not having to remember what lies we told
   -- experiencing less arguing and fighting, less stress
   -- having higher self-esteem, feeling freer to enjoy life
   -- having healthier relationships and communication

16. In what ways have you been **assertive**? What have been the benefits and negative consequences?

Example: Lauren kept quiet around her parents for many years. Then she took a series of communication skills classes and started speaking up with her parents when she disagreed with them. She practiced asking for what she needed, using "I" statements, and setting boundaries.

Her negative consequences were that her parents felt threatened by her at first, because she no longer went along with whatever they said. She also felt nervous and uncomfortable around them for awhile, and worried that they would see her as selfish. There were several uncomfortable dinners and holidays in the first few months.

Her benefits have been that over time, she's built a reputation among her entire extended family for being honest and straightforward. Her parents began to ask her what she thought about things, and their relationship improved because they got to know her better. She now has much more of what she wants in her life, and less of what she doesn't want.

Your example and consequences (both negative and positive):

17. When you're not being assertive, which communication style do you use most often?

    aggressive   passive   passive-aggressive

18. In what ways do you want to be more assertive? How do you think things will change for the better when you make these changes?

Now What?

Now it's all a matter of practice. I would suggest choosing one behavior to work on at a time, such as making more "I" statements or asking directly for what you want or need. Practice it regularly for three or four weeks, until it becomes easier and more automatic. Then choose another assertive behavior and practice it. After awhile, assertiveness will become a habit, and the benefits will begin coming your way.

The first assertive behavior I will practice is: _____

and I will start on the following date: _____

Is It Yours Yet?

Be prepared to answer (either verbally or in writing) the following questions about communication styles.

1. Give a brief description of what it means to be aggressive.
2. What are the basic benefits and consequences of being aggressive?
3. Give a brief description of what it means to be passive.
4. What are the basic benefits and consequences of being passive?
5. Give a brief description of what it means to be passive-aggressive.
6. What are the basic benefits and consequences of being passive-aggressive?
7. Give a brief description of what it means to be assertive.
8. What are the basic benefits and consequences of being assertive?

TOOL #8: SETTING HEALTHY BOUNDARIES

Overview:

Learn what healthy boundaries are, why we need them, and how to clearly set and maintain them. Use the step-by-step process to stand up for yourself and keep your power, even if the other person doesn't cooperate.

Getting Started:

Think of a person you often find yourself getting annoyed with, and then think about the behaviors that person does that are most annoying. Chances are, these are boundary violations.

Example:

Elisabeth worked in a newspaper office one summer with a man whose favorite response to everything was, "Whatever!" It wasn't said in a friendly way; he was sarcastic and dismissive to everyone, especially anyone who corrected him or his work. He also had a habit (this is gross, but a relevant example) of picking his nose and wiping it on the bottom of his desk. Needless to say, they didn't spend a lot of time together.

Your Example:

Information on Boundaries:

Boundaries are limits we set in order to protect ourselves or to feel safe and comfortable. We also set boundaries around our own behavior (called containment boundaries) so that we don't violate or offend other people.

Boundaries are **not** about judging behaviors as "right" and "wrong." They're about comfort and discomfort, and respecting yourself and the people around you.

Here are the main categories of boundaries (many of them overlap), and examples of typical behaviors that may be perceived as violations:

Physical:

-- sitting too close
-- hugging without permission
-- tickling, practical jokes
-- pushing someone into water
-- coming in without knocking
-- borrowing without permission

-- poking, pushing, shoving
-- hitting, kicking, etc.
-- getting up in someone's face
-- standing too close
-- reading journals, letters
-- listening in on phone calls

Verbal:

-- threats
-- name calling
-- gossip
-- interrupting
-- insult, then "just kidding"
-- yelling

-- profanity
-- lying
-- blaming (verbal & emotional)
-- sarcasm
-- tone of voice, whining
-- speaking for group, not self

Emotional:

-- breaking a promise
-- lying (also verbal)
-- shaming (also verbal)
-- telling someone how to feel
-- mind games
-- being condescending
-- "smothering" behavior

-- cheating on someone
-- silent treatment
-- dirty looks
-- shoulds
-- making fun of others' feelings
-- avoiding someone

Sexual:

-- rape
-- touching without permission
-- sexual nicknames
-- whistling, catcalls
-- "rating" a person by number (she's a 10!)
-- talking to a woman's chest instead of her face
-- being possessive of another person

-- molestation
-- treating someone as an object
-- sexual talk, dirty jokes
-- ignoring a "no"

Spiritual:

-- criticizing or harassing someone about beliefs or religious affiliation
-- staring, dirty looks, etc., as a response to spiritual clothing or jewelry such as robes, turbans, Star of David, etc.
-- vandalizing or mocking spiritual symbols (burning crosses or hanging them upside down, spray painting swastikas, etc.)
-- any comments indicating that a person is "nothing" or "worthless"

Boundaries As A Personal Issue:

As you read the preceding list, you may have found items there that don't particularly offend you. For instance, one physical boundary that varies widely from person to person is being tickled. You may hate it, like it, or not really care, which is probably dependent on your experiences of being tickled as a kid. In the verbal category, profanity is another issue that varies widely. Some people are deeply offended by it; others more neutral, and some enjoy it and use it regularly.

The point is not to decide who's right or wrong, but to determine your own comfort level and ask for your choices to be respected.

1. Look back at the list of boundary violations, and list which violations in each category personally bother you the most.

Physical:

Verbal:

Emotional:

Sexual:

Spiritual:

2. Which category or categories of boundaries have been violated the most often in your life, and who did the violating?

3. Which category or categories of boundaries have you violated the most often in your life, and whose boundaries have you violated?

Setting Boundaries:

We set boundaries every day, whether we realize it or not. Turning off the TV or changing the channel is boundary setting. So is screening phone calls, saying "no" to sales people, and closing the door to tune out loud music (or turning up the music to tune out loud parents). On the more aggressive side, one sixth grader bullying another, and the second one finally punching the first one in the mouth to stop the teasing is also boundary setting.

The goal here is to learn to set boundaries in a healthy and assertive way, partly out of respect, and partly because it's most effective that way in the long run. Yelling "Shut up!" may be effective in the short run, but setting an assertive boundary will have a more positive long-term effect. There are also places where yelling "Shut up!" will get you fired, hit, suspended, or grounded, and healthy boundary setting bypasses those consequences.

Many times you can set a healthy boundary informally, such as saying, "Ouch," when someone steps on your foot, or "Can you pay me back by Thursday?" when someone owes you money. However, there are times when simple, informal boundaries aren't enough, and you'll need a more structured process to completely settle an issue.

On the following page is an assertive boundary setting structure that works extremely well when informal boundaries aren't enough. It will probably feel awkward at first, and it definitely takes practice, but it does work:

THE BOUNDARY SETTING PROCESS

STEP 1: The "I" Statement

"When you..."

(Describe the specific behavior; no judgment words.)

"I feel..."

(Feeling words only; no "feel like" or "feel that.")

STEP 2: The Request for Change

"My request is..."

(Make a specific request, not just "stop it.")

STEP 3: Asking for a Commitment

"Will you agree to that?"

(Compromise if needed, but end with a definite yes or no.)

STEP 4: Stating a Consequence*

"I need to tell you that if this doesn't change, I will take care of myself by..."

*(Use this step only if the other person won't agree to your request, or agrees but continues to violate the boundary. Be careful of threats, and only state a consequence that you are actually willing to follow through with.)

<u>Examples</u>:

First, here's an example of an unproductive, attacking way to set a boundary:

"Jason, I need to talk to you about something. When you act like a jerk, I feel like hurting you, and my request is that you get your act together before I do something we both regret.

Will you agree to that?

I need to tell you that if this doesn't change, I guarantee that I won't be an easy person to be around."

There are several problems with this boundary. "Jerk" is a judgment word, and it doesn't describe what Jason's behavior is -- he may not even know what he's doing, so this doesn't help. "Feel like" is a thought, not a feeling, and "feel like hurting you" is an underhanded form of intimidation or implied threat. The request of "get your act together" doesn't ask Jason to do anything specific, and "I guarantee that I won't be an easy person to be around" isn't even implied -- it's an outright threat.

Here's an alternative to that boundary, which would be more healthy and productive:

"Jason, I need to talk to you about something: When you borrow my clothes and CDs without asking, and then leave them on the floor, I feel aggravated and frustrated. My request is that you ask before using anything of mine, and if you do use things with my permission, please take care of them and put them away when you're done with them.

Will you agree to that?

I need to tell you that if this doesn't change, I will take care of myself by not letting you use anything of mine, and if you do, I'll install a lock on my bedroom door."

Here are two more examples of healthy, appropriate use of this format:

1. "John, I need to talk to you about something. When you tell me I shouldn't be afraid, I feel shame, hurt, and fear. My request is that you listen while I express whatever feelings I'm having without telling me any 'shoulds.'

Will you agree to that?

I need to tell you that if this doesn't change, I will take care of myself by reminding you about not using 'shoulds,' and if you keep using them, I'll leave the conversation."

2. *"Robin, I need to talk to you about something. When you agree to meet me at a certain time, and then are 30 minutes late, I feel angry and hurt. My request is that you follow through on what we planned, and that if you're going to be late, you call me to let me know.*

Will you agree to that?

I need to tell you that if this doesn't change, I will take care of myself by waiting fifteen minutes, then I'll either leave or go on by myself with whatever we had planned."

Your Turn:

Choose two of the following situations, and write sample boundaries for both. This will help you get more comfortable with the format.

A. Someone repeatedly interrupts you.
B. Someone reads your journal or letters.
C. Someone stands too close while talking to you.
D. Someone tickles you and you don't like it.
E. Someone hugs or touches you without permission.
F. Someone walks away in the middle of your sentence.
G. Someone calls you by a nickname you don't like.

1. _____, I need to talk to you about something:

When you _____,

I feel _____. My request is _____

_____.

Will you agree to that?

I need to tell you that if this doesn't change, I will take care of myself by

_____

_____.

2. _____, I need to talk to you about something:

When you _____,

I feel _____. My request is _____

_____.

Will you agree to that?

I need to tell you that if this doesn't change, I will take care of myself by

_____

_____.

Now think of several situations (current if possible, past if there aren't too many current ones) from your own life, and write out healthy boundaries that you could set with those involved.

_____, I need to talk to you about something:

When you _____,

I feel _____. My request is _____

_____.

Will you agree to that?

I need to tell you that if this doesn't change, I will take care of myself by

_____

_____.

- - - - - - - - - - - - - - - -

_____, I need to talk to you about something:

When you _____,

I feel _____. My request is _____

_____.

Will you agree to that?

I need to tell you that if this doesn't change, I will take care of myself by

_____

_____.

- - - - - - - - - - - - - -

_____, I need to talk to you about something:

When you _____,

I feel _____. My request is _____

_____.

Will you agree to that?

I need to tell you that if this doesn't change, I will take care of myself by

_____

_____.

- - - - - - - - - - - - - -

Some IMPORTANT Notes About Boundary Setting:

The first thing is that **safety** is key in boundary setting. If you believe that a person you want to set a boundary with may hit you or otherwise harm you, don't set the boundary, or at least don't do it alone.

For example: If I work at a convenience store on the night shift, and someone comes in and points a gun at me, I am not going to say, "Sir (or Ma'am), I need to talk to you about something. When you point that gun at me, I feel distinctly uncomfortable, and my request is that you put the gun away. Will you agree to that?" etc. If I do that, I'm probably going to get shot, and no boundary is worth that. Realistically, my most likely response in that situation would be, "Would you like that in tens and twenties? Can I put them in a nice sturdy bag for you?"

Another thing to realize is that boundary setting is not a neat and tidy process, no matter how skilled you are at it. Most people don't enjoy being called on their inappropriate behavior, and some will get angry or defensive when you set a boundary. This doesn't mean you did it wrong. You may get laughed at or scoffed at, but you will have stood up for yourself and spoken your truth. Some people will agree to respect your boundary and then forget, and need to be reminded. Others will agree to respect your boundary and then deliberately ignore it. That's why Step 4 exists.

I remember being really surprised (and not very happy) when I realized that hinting around about boundaries wasn't going to work, and that I was actually going to have to speak up and ask directly for what I needed. I hoped for many years that people (especially those closest to me) would have common sense and common courtesy, and intuitively know what I needed and what was respectful. Not likely.

I was also surprised (and even less happy) to realize that I was going to have to set the same boundaries repeatedly with certain people in my life, and that the really difficult part isn't just setting the boundaries, it's **maintaining** them -- speaking up or saying "no" repeatedly on the same issue, and following through with whatever I said I was going to do in Step 4. I'm still working on that.

Women in particular have been trained to be polite and please others, and setting and maintaining boundaries can feel deeply uncomfortable. Boundary work takes constant practice; you will most likely make mistakes and do it badly sometimes. Oh well -- welcome to the imperfect human race. I encourage you to set boundaries anyway, and to know that it does get easier over time.

What If I'm The One Violating Boundaries?

First of all, good for you if you've realized this is your issue. It takes courage to acknowledge that, even to yourself. Here are some tips for practicing containment boundaries:

1. Let people in your life know that you're aware of this issue, and working on it. Ask them to remind you politely when they see you doing things that are violating. Give them a neutral "cue word" or phrase to say to you, such as, "Boundaries," or "There's that boundary thing," and say thank you when they remind you.

2. If you find yourself violating boundaries when you're angry, practice using the earlier tools you've learned, especially "What's Under Anger" and "The Rage Bomb," so you can diffuse the anger and stay respectful.

3. Start looking for and paying attention to body language and other subtle signals. For instance, if people say you stand too close to them, start watching their faces for cues, such as noticing that they can't keep eye contact with you, or that they turn away, lean back, or back away. With practice, you can pick up on these cues and adjust your behaviors. You can do it -- don't give up.

Now What?

As usual, practice. First, write out several boundaries you would like to set with others (you can make copies of the blank worksheet on page 101), even if you never really intend to set them. Then practice out loud alone. Then practice out loud with someone you trust. Then decide if you actually want to set the boundary, and whether you want to bring someone along with you for support.

Also, feel free to take your written boundary with you and even read it from the page when you set it if you need to. That helps to keep you from getting side tracked or forgetting the wonderful wording you came up with. It won't be the most suave and sophisticated thing you ever do in your life, but again, you will have stood up for yourself, which fires up some powerful self-respect. Keep practicing -- it will definitely get easier.

Is It Yours Yet?

Be prepared to answer (either verbally or in writing) the following questions about setting healthy boundaries.

1. What are boundaries and why do we need them?
2. What is the difference between protective boundaries and containment boundaries?
3. Name the five general categories of boundary violations.
4. If boundaries aren't about "right" and "wrong" behaviors, what are they about?
5. Why does assertive boundary setting work better than passive (such as hinting) or aggressive (such as yelling "Shut up!") boundary setting?
6. Name the four steps of setting a healthy, assertive boundary.
7. What do we need to particularly avoid during the fourth step?
8. What is the first consideration we need to make when deciding whether or not to set a boundary with someone? (See the convenience store example.)
9. Why is it important for us to set boundaries even if the other person ignores them, laughs at us, and doesn't honor the boundaries?
10. After setting particular boundaries, why is it so important to maintain them?

TOOL #9 -- THE DRAMA TRIANGLE

(This information is adapted from Stephen Karpman's original work, copyright 1968.)

Overview:

Learn the unproductive roles people play in most conflicts, how to identify which roles you and others are playing, and how to get out of the triangle and stay balanced, no matter what anyone else is doing.

Getting Started:

Think of someone you know who does one or more of the following on a regular basis: blames everything on other people, whines or tries to elicit pity from others, uses guilt trips or other manipulation to get his/her way, and/or tries to fix everyone else's lives and ignores his or her own issues.

Example:

Tom and Amy are both 18, and have been together for two years. Tom has a lot of family problems, especially with his dad. He drinks with his friends and cheats on Amy, then blames other girls for approaching him when he's drinking, and blames Amy for not being there for him enough. Amy keeps trying to fix him and all his problems, and whenever she gets fed up and decides to leave the relationship, he manipulates her by falling apart and telling her he couldn't live without her, and talks her into coming back.

Your Example:

About The Drama Triangle:

The Drama Triangle is a pattern that many people get into when they're in conflict and don't know how to be assertive. It usually happens between two people, but it can happen with more, or even with one person alone. This dynamic is based on denial, blaming, guilt trips, and other imbalances of power. When people are in these unproductive roles, the conflict becomes a mind game where everyone loses.

There are three main roles in the Drama Triangle, and one role people can play in order to leave the triangle:

IMPORTANT NOTE: Just about everyone has played each one of these roles at one time or another. <u>This information is intended to raise awareness, not to label.</u> PLEASE use this information in a productive way, rather than to categorize or judge others.

The Drama Triangle

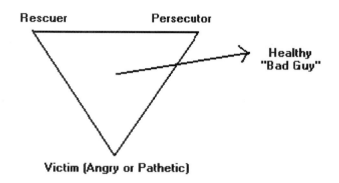

The "Victim" Role:

The Drama Triangle revolves around the person playing the "victim" role. This person is not an actual victim, but someone who sees himself as a victim. People playing the victim role take no responsibility for their actions or feelings.

> *"It's your fault I hit you, because you made me mad."*
> *"I wouldn't have to drink if my boss wasn't such a jerk."*
> *"She gets me so depressed I can't think straight."*

People playing the victim role blame others for their problems.

> *"My life is a mess because of him."*
> *"If you'd never been born, my life would be perfect."*
> *"You caused all the problems in this family."*

People playing the victim role insist that they are stuck.

> *"That's just the way I am."*

"I can't change, and if you say I can, you don't understand."
"I've tried everything and nothing works."

Those in the victim role are either **angry** (blaming & raging) or acting **pathetic** (poor me), and they can switch back and forth if one tactic isn't working. They manipulate others into feeling sorry for them, or into feeling guilty. They look for someone (a rescuer) who will take care of things for them, and who they can blame when things go wrong.

<u>Sample situations with a strong victim role component</u>:

-- An alcoholic or addict who blames his or her substance abuse on others.
-- Someone who physically or emotionally abuses a partner and then blames the partner for "making" him or her do it.
-- A spouse who cheats on his or her partner, and then blames the partner for causing the problem.
-- An employee who is consistently late or does poor work, and blames traffic, the broken alarm clock, the spouse, the broken down car, the computer, etc., for every mistake or problem.
-- A person with chronic aches and pains or illness who believes he or she is totally powerless and blames rude or abusive behavior on the illness.

1. When have you played the victim role? Give examples.

2. Who else do you know who plays the victim role? Give examples.

<u>The Rescuer Role</u>:

People playing the rescuer role look like "good guys" who help other people solve their problems.

"I just enjoy helping others. What's wrong with that?"
"I feel good about myself when I help someone else."
"I like to feel needed. It's just the way I am."
"I help people out because I'm a good friend."
"I'm just a very caring person."

People playing the rescuer role jump in to fix the situation when someone else is struggling.

"When he hurts, I hurt too."
"I hate to see people cry. I want them to feel better."
"He didn't know the answer. What's wrong with me saying it?"
"What she meant to say was..."

The problem with the rescuer role is that people playing it are focusing on others instead of on themselves, and they avoid their own feelings, needs, and issues. People playing the rescuer role are also making themselves needed so they will not be abandoned. This is a dishonest and manipulative way to connect with another person.

The person being rescued is not allowed to feel his own pain, make his own mistakes, or deal with his own consequences. Therefore, that person is unlikely to grow and move forward. Those in the rescuer role make excuses for the unproductive behavior of the person in the victim role, and make it easier for that person to avoid the truth.

"I see that you have to drink because your boss is a jerk."
"I know you had to hit me. I shouldn't have made you mad."
"I know you can't help it. You've had such a rough life."
"You're right. Nobody understands what you've been through."

Those playing the rescuer role often place themselves above others. They give the message, "You can't help yourself, but I can help you." Eventually the person in the victim role will get tired of being controlled and will object. Then the person playing the rescuer will feel abused and become a "victim" too:

"After all I've done for you, this is how you thank me."

<u>How to tell whether we're RESCUING or SUPPORTING</u>:

Sometimes there's a fine line between the two. If we're thinking of helping someone out, and are not sure whether we're rescuing or supporting that person, we can ask ourselves two questions:

A. Is the person **able** to do this for himself/herself?   AND
B. Would it in some way **benefit** the person to do this for himself/herself?

If the answer to **both** questions is **yes**, then we're rescuing the person. If the answer to **either one** is **no**, then we're not rescuing. Consider the following situations:

-- A mother giving money to her 10-year-old daughter for school lunch.

> A) No, the ten-year-old isn't reasonably able to pay for her own lunch.
> B) No, it wouldn't particularly benefit the ten-year-old to pay for her own lunch.

-- The same woman giving lunch money to her adult partner because he chooses to work part time so he doesn't miss his favorite TV shows, and has no money.

> A) Yes, he is able to work and pay for his own lunches.
> B) Yes, it would probably benefit him to provide his own lunch money.

-- The same woman giving lunch money to her adult partner while he launches a new business and is temporarily short on cash.

> A) Yes, he could probably figure out a way to pay for his own lunches.
> B) No, it isn't necessarily beneficial to him, unless this is the 8th business he's started in the past two years and he's clearly taking advantage.

<u>Sample situations with a strong rescuer role component:</u>

-- The partner of an alcoholic or addict, physically or emotionally abusive partner, or cheating spouse, who accepts the behavior and takes the blame, enables the partner to continue the unproductive behavior, and stays in the relationship even when it's harmful or dangerous.

-- The indulgent parents or other family members of that addict or abusive person, who supply living expenses, buy the person cars, pay bills when they're overdue, etc., even further enabling the person to continue his or her destructive behaviors.

-- A boss or supervisor who accepts the behavior of an employee who is consistently late or does poor work and always has an excuse. This looks like "helping out" or "supporting" the employee in the short run, but in the long run it's damaging to everyone involved.

-- The parents of a student who doesn't do work, ditches class, and is consistently disrespectful to adults, and the parents say, "He can't help it because _____," "We don't believe in homework," "He's just being a kid," or (my personal favorite) "You must be mistaken -- my child would never do anything like that."

3. When have you played the rescuer role? Give examples.

4. Who else do you know who plays the rescuer role ? Give examples.

The Persecutor Role:

The person in the persecutor role comes across as condescending, arrogant, superior, often sarcastic, know-it-all, and tries to "win" and be in control in all situations and conflicts.

> *"I know this is probably beyond you, but I'll try to explain it in a way you can understand."*

Those playing the Persecutor role are judgmental and punishing.

> *"You just don't get it, do you?"*
> *"She knows better than to talk to me that way."*
> *"I'll talk to you when you're ready to listen to reason."*

Those playing the persecutor role present themselves as experts on many topics. They enjoy debates focusing on who's right and wrong. They rarely admit making any mistakes, and are very emotionally invested in being right, and in having everyone else agree. They also pride themselves on staying in control emotionally at all times, and will exert control over anyone who will let them.

People playing the persecutor role may have excellent manners and be very smooth and articulate. They may seem friendly and open, until someone disagrees with them. Even then, the debates may be polite, but those in the persecutor role rarely give up until the argument is won, and then they may come across as smug or superior.

Situations with a strong persecutor component:

-- A teacher or boss giving instructions to a student or employee in a rude or condescending way.
-- An expert in some area giving a lecture on a topic and using unnecessarily big or complicated terms to sound superior, especially if the vocabulary suddenly gets more complex when someone asks a challenging question.
-- A person losing an argument who says, "Well, obviously you don't understand, so it's not worth continuing this discussion."
-- A person who's been in the Rescuer role and finally gets fed up, saying something like, "Fine -- you obviously can't be helped, so never mind."
-- A person with strong religious beliefs making negative assumptions or judgments about someone with differing beliefs.

5. When have you played the persecutor role? Give examples.

6. Who else do you know who plays the persecutor role? Give examples.

The "Healthy Bad Guy" Role:

The healthy bad guy role is the only way out of the drama triangle. It is impossible to get out while playing the victim, rescuer, or persecutor roles.

The Bad Guy is really the Healthy Guy, but to those in the other roles, he looks like the bad guy because he speaks directly and honestly, assertively challenges the lies, denial, manipulation, and blaming, using "I" statements and setting healthy boundaries.

The bottom line is that in order to get out of the Drama Triangle, a person has to have the courage to tell the truth and be willing to look like the bad guy to other people, in order to stop the unproductive cycle of the triangle and the conflict. The healthy bad guy is actually more helpful, and a more truly supportive friend, than the person in the rescuer role (who appears helpful, but is actually enabling the other person).

The healthy bad guy role is what you've been learning to play throughout this workbook. All of the tools and skills you've learned and practiced so far are preparing you for the healthy bad guy role if you choose to play it.

7. In what ways do you play the healthy bad guy role?

8. In what situations do you have trouble staying in this role?

9. When you aren't in the healthy bad guy role, which other role do you play most often?

10. What healthy bad guy behaviors do you most need to practice in order to be more productive or more balanced?

Becoming More Familiar With The Roles:

One of the easiest ways to identify Drama Triangle Roles is to use characters from TV shows or movies. You may be more familiar with some of these shows than other (and you may agree or disagree with my take on the characters), but hopefully it will give you the general idea:

WINNIE THE POOH:

Victim Role: Pooh, Piglet, Eeyore
Rescuer Role: Christopher Robin?
Persecutor Role: Rabbit, Owl
Healthy Bad Guy Role: Kanga, Roo

THE ANDY GRIFFITH SHOW:

Victim Role: Barney, Howard Sprague's mother
Rescuer Role: Andy (usually with Barney), Howard
Persecutor Role: Barney, Aunt Bee
Healthy Bad Guy Role: Opie, sometimes Andy

FRASIER:

Victim Role: Niles
Rescuer Role: Frasier, Daphne
Persecutor Role: Martin, Roz, Frasier, Niles
Healthy Bad Guy Role: Daphne, sometimes Frasier, sometimes Martin

I LOVE LUCY:

Victim Role: Lucy
Rescuer Role: Ethel, sometimes Lucy
Persecutor Role: Ricky, Fred
Healthy Bad Guy Role: Haven't seen one yet!

You choose a TV show or movie: _____

Victim Role:

Rescuer Role:

Persecutor Role:

Healthy Bad Guy Role:

Now What?

Now you can start paying attention when you're in conflict with someone, or when you're around people in conflict. Remember that it's not about labeling or judging, but awareness. If you're involved in the conflict, pay attention to **your own** behavior, and see if you're playing one of the unproductive roles. If you are, think about what you would need to say or do to switch to the healthy bad guy role, no matter what anyone else is doing. Do you need to start using "I" statements? Do you need to set a boundary? Do you need to take a break and write out a "What's Under Anger" or "Rage Bomb" sheet so you can come back and work toward actually resolving the issue?

I do NOT recommend saying to someone else, "You're just being a pathetic victim today, and you need to do something about it!" First of all, those aren't "I" statements, and second, the chances of this leading anywhere productive are slim to none. You may want to teach people in your life about the Drama Triangle, but not in the heat of an argument. My encouragement to you is to focus on your own behaviors first, and work your way out of the triangle. When you're firmly planted in the healthy bad guy role, you may want to approach the people around you with this tool. If it can't wait that long, I would encourage you to talk to a counselor, and if your partner or family members are willing, get them into a counseling session so you can all work on it together with a facilitator. As with all the other tools you're learning: Practice, more practice, and don't give up.

Is It Yours Yet?

Be prepared to answer (either verbally or in writing) the following questions about the Drama Triangle.

1. What is the Drama Triangle, and why is it a useful concept to be aware of?
2. Give a basic description or an example of someone playing the victim role.
3. What are the two categories of victim role?

4. What are the biggest drawbacks or consequences to the victim role?
5. Give a basic description or an example of someone playing the rescuer role.
6. What are the two questions we can ask to determine whether we're rescuing or supporting another person?
7. What are the biggest drawbacks or consequences to the rescuer role?
8. Give a basic description or an example of someone playing the persecutor role.
9. What are the biggest drawbacks or consequences to the persecutor role?
10. Give a basic description or an example of someone playing the healthy bad guy role.
11. Why is it called the "healthy bad guy" role?
12. What are the biggest drawbacks and benefits to the healthy bad guy role?

TOOL #10: HEALTHY OUTLETS FOR ANGER & STRESS

Overview:

Learn what separates healthy venting from being destructive or harmful, and identify dozens of healthy outlets (in several different categories) that you can use when you're angry or stressed.

Getting Started:

Think of at least one thing you do when you're angry or stressed that you believe is unhealthy or unproductive, and at least one thing you do that's healthy or productive.

Examples:

On the healthy/productive side, Jessie talks with supportive friends, writes journal entries and poetry, uses the ten tools, goes off by herself and bawls her head off while yelling out loud at whoever she's angry with, takes walks, does yoga, plays volleyball, reads good fiction, and meditates.

On the unhealthy/unproductive side, she gets sarcastic, still occasionally throws things (generally nothing breakable, and not in front of anyone), yells at people from time to time, and occasionally still keeps quiet when she needs to speak up.

Your Examples:

Healthy/productive:

Unhealthy/unproductive:

Healthy Venting vs. Destructive Expression of Feelings:

The definition of "healthy" that we'll use in regard to venting and expressing feelings is that A) we feel better after we do it, B) no one is harmed, physically or emotionally, including us, and C) it either involves "moving" emotions through our systems (physically, verbally, or creatively), or it gives us a break and a chance to calm down and get some perspective. Needless to say, having several choices available is a good idea.

On the following page is a checklist of healthy ways to vent or release anger or stress. Fill it out and then make two or three copies of it, so you can keep one at school or work, one in your purse or backpack, and one in your bedroom or kitchen (post it on the refrigerator). That way, you always have the list available. When you're stressed or angry, you may not be thinking clearly, and may not be able to think of even one healthy stress reliever. If you keep a copy of the list on the refrigerator, you can refer to it whenever you get really frustrated, pick an activity and do it, and then pick another one, and another one, until you feel calm enough to stop.

Also, please be aware that some of the things on this list will be appropriate at some times and places, but not at others. For instance, throwing ice or destroying a cardboard box would probably not be allowed at school or work. And if your methods of venting are intense (crying, yelling, etc.), be aware of children in the area (so you don't scare or traumatize them) and let someone else in your household know what you're going to do, so no one calls the police when they hear hysterical screaming.

Personal Plan for Anger and Stress Relief:

Directions: Circle what you already do. Box what you might try.

1. PHYSICAL ACTIVITY: bike riding   skating or roller blading   skateboarding   walking   hiking   basketball   baseball   football   hockey   soccer   volleyball   swimming   dance   weights   working out   martial arts   other: _____

2. TALKING WITH SOMEONE: mom   dad   brother   sister   grandma   grandpa   aunt   uncle   cousin   other relative   friends   teacher   neighbor   counselor   minister   dog   cat   other pet   teddy bear   prayer   other: _____

3. HEALTHY COMMUNICATION: set boundaries   speak your truth   be assertive   be honest   keep promises   ask for what you need   use "I" statements   follow through   say "no" when you need to   admit mistakes   give your opinion   listen to all sides   be direct   give feedback instead of advice   say what you feel

4. WRITING/ART/MUSIC: letters   journal   stories   poems   drawing   scribbling   painting   coloring   pottery   sculpture   jewelry making   photography   crafts   scrapbooking   singing   playing an instrument   other: _____

5. BUILDING/MAKING THINGS: _____

6. CLUBS/PROJECTS/COLLECTIONS: _____

7. RELAXATION: stretches   deep breathing   meditation   yoga   count to 10   backrubs   muscle relaxation   rest/sleep   TV   movies   music   reading   other: _____

8. NATURE: camping   fishing   hiking   walking   exploring   gardening

9. VENTING*: cry   scream   throw ice   hit bed with a pillow   scream into a pillow   scream in the shower   destroy a box   batting cages   hammer nails   throw unbreakable things   loud music   write unsent letters   punching bag   tetherball   hug someone   throw rocks in the desert   other: _____

Ten Real Tools For Real Life by Susan Hansen, M.S. copyright 2002, 2006. All Rights Reserved.

*Notes About The Venting Activities:

Most of these activities are self-explanatory, but I want to say more about two of them. "Destroy a box" was an idea given to me by a 4th grader at one of the schools where I worked as a counselor. When he was really angry, he would take an old empty cardboard box and write or draw on it all the things he was angry about or hated, or he would imagine the person he was angry with inside the box. Then he would kick, stomp on, and otherwise trash the box until all that was left were little pieces. He threw the pieces away, and that was the end of that. I've used that activity with clients of all ages, and have done it myself, and it really is satisfying. My only cautions are to make sure you have enough space to kick and stomp without accidentally breaking anything else, and if you need to, let someone know what you're doing ahead of time.

"Throw ice" was an idea given to me by a 7th grader at the same school. He liked to break things when he was angry, but didn't like the consequences. He found that throwing ice gave him the same satisfaction because it was heavy, solid, and it shattered loudly and dramatically when he threw it at the block fence in his back yard. Sometimes he used ice cubes out of the tray, and sometimes he made bigger "ice bombs" by filling up Ziploc bags with water and freezing them for a few days. With the usual cautions (not around younger kids, pets, windows, etc.), this can be a powerful way to release anger, with no damage done and nothing to clean up (the ice just melts).

Now What?

Basically, keep your list handy, and when you're stressed, choose something on the list and do it. If you're still stressed, do another one, and do as many as you need until you either feel calmer, or are exhausted and can go to sleep for awhile. Do a variety of activities -- some physical, some verbal, some creative, etc. -- and after awhile you'll get a clearer sense of what works best for you in different situations. The great thing is that you'll always have several choices in front of you. I once read that the person who sees the most options is the person with the best mental health. I don't know if I believe that as an absolute rule, but I think it's true for most people, most of the time.

Is It Yours Yet?

Be prepared to answer (either verbally or in writing) the following questions about healthy outlets for anger and stress.

1. What are the three components of healthy venting?
2. Why is it a good idea to make up an extensive list of possible activities in advance?

NOW THAT YOU'VE STOCKED YOUR TOOLBOX...

CONGRATULATIONS! If you've had the courage to complete all the activities in this workbook, you now have more tools and more skills for creating and maintaining emotional health than most people will ever have.

You've gone from a student or apprentice to a journeyman. Now all there is to do is USE THE TOOLS on a regular basis and hone your skills. As you become more experienced and practiced with them, you'll use them more easily and automatically, and you won't have to think about the steps. In the meantime, keep this workbook where you can refer to it. There are blank copies of several of the worksheets on the following pages, so you can make your own copies and use these tools whenever you need them.

If you'd like more tools or more structured practice, I would encourage you to find and join a support group, work with a counselor, or go on to the other workbooks which will soon be available in this series -- one for dealing with grief and loss, and another for healing through writing. Check out the *Ten Real Tools for Real Life* web page at:

 www.trafford.com/robots/02-0608.html

You can also find the original *Tools For Your Emotional Health Toolbox* on Trafford at:

www.trafford.com/robots/04-02082.html

Also, please check out my school counseling website at:

www.schoolcounselingcommunity.com

This site is for school counselors and other educators, parents, and students, and contains hundreds of links chosen with the mental and emotional health of students in mind.

I wish you the best on your journey, wherever it may lead you, and I hope these tools have helped you come to know yourself better, and have equipped you more fully for dealing with tension, feelings, conflict, and other interactions with the people in your life.

Take care, and I wish you true peace!

Susan Hansen :)
August 2002, Phoenix, AZ

BLANK COPIES OF WORKSHEETS
FOR YOUR CONTINUED USE

<u>CHECK-IN</u>:

Today's Date: _____

1. A low point for me was _____

_____...

2. ... and I felt _____.

3. A high point for me was _____

_____...

4. ... and I felt _____.

~   ~   ~   ~   ~   ~   ~   ~   ~   ~   ~   ~   ~

Today's Date: _____

1. A low point for me was _____

_____...

2. ... and I felt _____.

3. A high point for me was _____

_____...

4. ... and I felt _____.

~   ~   ~   ~   ~   ~   ~   ~   ~   ~   ~   ~   ~

Today's Date: _____

1. A low point for me was _____

_____...

2. ... and I felt _____.

3. A high point for me was _____

_____...

4. ... and I felt _____.

WHAT'S UNDER ANGER

1. The situation is...

2. I'm angry because...

3. I'm hurt because...

4. My fear is...

5. I wish...

6. I want...

7. I need...

8. I accept...

9. I understand...

10. To take care of myself in this situation, I'm going to...

"RAGE BOMB" WORKSHEET -- Diffusing the Bomb

1. What was the situation you raged about?

2. What act of rage did you do?

3. Fill in the following statements:

I felt **angry** because:

I felt **hurt** because:

I felt **fear** because:

I felt **shame/powerless** because:

4. What could you do in the future to take care of yourself instead of raging?

RAGE PREVENTION WORKSHEET

1. What is the situation that you feel like raging about?

2. What do you feel like doing, that you have to hold yourself back from?

3. Fill in the following statements:

I'm **angry** because:

I'm **hurt** because:

My **fear** is:

I feel **shame/powerless** because:

4. What is one healthy way you can take care of yourself instead of raging?

BOUNDARY SETTING PRACTICE

_____, I need to talk to you about something:

When you _____,

I feel _____. My request is _____

_____.

Will you agree to that?

I need to tell you that if this doesn't change, I will take care of myself by

_____

_____.

- - - - - - - - - - - - -

_____, I need to talk to you about something:

When you _____,

I feel _____. My request is _____

_____.

Will you agree to that?

I need to tell you that if this doesn't change, I will take care of myself by

_____

_____.

CONTACT INFORMATION:

If you have questions about the workbook or the activities, or would like to contact Susan about individual coaching sessions, speaking engagements, workshops, or support group facilitator trainings, please visit her website at www.schoolcounselingcommunity.com , call her at 602-488-0275, or write to her at:

Susan Hansen
2525 W. Greenway Rd.
Suite 124
Phoenix, AZ 85023

- -

ADDITIONAL WORKBOOKS:

To order additional copies of this workbook, please visit the Trafford website at www.trafford.com (on the home page, click "Enter the Bookstore") or visit the *Ten Real Tools For Real Life* page on Trafford's site at www.trafford.com/robots/02-0608.html . You can also place a phone order by calling Trafford Publishing toll free at 1-888-232-4444.

To learn about or order copies of *Tools For Your Emotional Health Toolbox*, which contains almost 300 pages of activities, lesson plans, and handouts that can be used by teachers, school counselors, group facilitators, therapists, or anyone else who has an interest in emotional health or personal growth, please visit the main Trafford website or place a phone order (see above), or visit the *Tools For Your Emotional Health Toolbox* page at www.trafford.com/robots/04-2082.html .

~ NOTES ~

ISBN 1553697954-2

9 781553 697954